UZBEKISTAN TRAVEL GUIDE 2023 2024

Unveiling Uzbekistan: Discover the Hidden Treasures of Central Asia's Enchanting Gem

ISLAND PRINCE J

Welcome to Uzbekistan

I embarked on a remarkable journey to explore the captivating wonders of Uzbekistan. With anticipation in my heart and a spirit of adventure, I arrived in Tashkent, the bustling capital city. The grandeur of the modern metropolis intertwined with glimpses of ancient history welcomed me with open arms.

In Tashkent, I immersed myself in the vibrant city life, strolling through the wide boulevards and admiring the futuristic architecture that coexisted harmoniously with traditional structures. The regal Amir Timur Square and the majestic Independence Square left me in awe of Uzbekistan's rich heritage.

From Tashkent, my journey led me to the enchanting city of Samarkand. As I entered the city, I was instantly transported back in time. The grandeur of Registan Square took my breath away, with its three magnificent madrasas adorned with intricate tile work and majestic domes. I marveled at the celestial beauty of the Ulugbek Observatory, a testament to the brilliance of medieval astronomy.

Next, I ventured into the ancient city of Bukhara, known as a living museum. The narrow winding streets of the old town, Shahristan, echoed with tales of the past. I explored the UNESCO World Heritage Sites, such as the Ark Fortress and the Po-i-Kalyan Complex, which held the secrets of centuries gone by. Bukhara's bustling bazaars captivated me with their vibrant colors and the aroma of spices, while the melodic tunes of traditional music floated through the air.

Leaving Bukhara, my journey took me to the fairy-tale city of Khiva. As I stepped into the walls of Ichan-Kala, the ancient inner city, I felt like a time traveler wandering through a bygone era. The intricate mosaic work of the Juma Mosque and the towering minaret of Islam Khodja transported me to a world of legends and folklore. I relished the warm hospitality of the locals, savoring traditional dishes and engaging in heartfelt conversations.

But my exploration didn't stop there. I ventured into other regions of Uzbekistan, each offering its own unique charm. In Nukus, I marveled at the masterpieces of the Savitsky Museum, home to an impressive collection of Russian avant-garde art. The Fergana Valley beckoned with its vibrant craftsmanship, where I witnessed the intricate process of silk weaving and ceramic pottery.

I ventured to Termez, an ancient city on the Silk Road, where I discovered archaeological treasures and absorbed the spiritual aura of the city's sacred sites. The majestic Tian Shan Mountains offered me the opportunity to embark on exhilarating outdoor adventures, from trekking to skiing, amidst breathtaking natural landscapes. I also experienced the haunting beauty of the Aral Sea, contemplating the environmental challenges it faces.

Throughout my journey, I marveled at the kindness and warmth of the Uzbek people. Their hospitality and genuine smiles created lasting memories. As I bid farewell to this land of wonders, I carried with me the imprints of a captivating journey through Uzbekistan, a tale to be shared with fellow travelers and wanderlust-filled souls.

And so, with a heart full of gratitude and a longing to return, I left Uzbekistan, knowing that its timeless allure would forever hold a special place in my traveler's heart.

Introduction

Welcome to the enchanting land of Uzbekistan, a country that stands as a testament to the glory of the ancient Silk Road. As you turn the pages of this travel guide, get ready to embark on a captivating journey through time and discover the jewels that await you in this mesmerizing corner of Central Asia.

Uzbekistan, with its rich history, diverse landscapes, and vibrant culture, has long been a destination that ignites the imagination of travelers. Step foot in this land, and you'll find yourself immersed in a tapestry of architectural marvels, ancient cities, and warm-hearted people who welcome you with open arms.

This travel guide aims to be your trusted companion as you navigate the treasures of Uzbekistan. It is a culmination of invaluable knowledge, insider tips, and heartfelt recommendations, crafted to ensure that you experience the very best this captivating country has to offer.

Begin your adventure in the heart of it all, Tashkent, the capital city that seamlessly blends tradition with modernity. Explore its bustling bazaars, awe-inspiring monuments, and vibrant arts scene. From there, let the Silk Road lead you to the breathtaking city of Samarkand, where the majestic Registan Square and Ulugbek Observatory will transport you back to a time of splendor and innovation.

Continue your journey to the living museum of Bukhara, where the narrow alleys of the old town whisper stories of traders, scholars, and mystics who once graced its streets. Lose yourself in the labyrinthine lanes of Khiva, a fairy-tale city frozen in time, where ornate palaces and towering minarets beckon you to step into the pages of history.

But Uzbekistan's wonders don't end there. Venture beyond the renowned cities to uncover the hidden gems that lie in wait. Discover the art collections of Nukus, soak in the natural beauty of the Fergana Valley, and find solace in the ancient city of Termez, nestled along the mighty Amu Darya River.

As you journey through this guidebook, you'll also delve into the country's rich culture, from the traditional arts and crafts that have been meticulously passed down through generations, to the vibrant music and dance that echo the melodies of the past. Learn about the customs, traditions, and warm hospitality of the Uzbek people, who will undoubtedly leave an indelible mark on your memories.

Whether you are a history enthusiast, an intrepid adventurer, or a curious traveler seeking to unravel the secrets of the Silk Road, Uzbekistan promises to captivate your senses and leave you longing for more. So, gather your wanderlust, embrace the spirit of exploration, and let this guidebook be your passport to an unforgettable journey through the Jewels of the Silk Road.

As you set foot on the soil of Uzbekistan, be prepared to lose yourself in a world where history comes alive, where the echoes of ancient caravans still resonate, and where the warmth of the people will make you feel like a cherished guest. May your travels be filled with wonder, discovery, and cherished memories that will last a lifetime.

Getting To Know Uzbekistan

Uzbekistan, located in Central Asia, is a landlocked country known for its rich history, cultural heritage, and stunning architectural marvels. It shares borders with Kazakhstan to the north, Tajikistan to the southeast, Kyrgyzstan to the northeast, Afghanistan to the south, and Turkmenistan to the southwest. The country is home to over 33 million people and its official language is Uzbek. Tashkent, the capital city, serves as the cultural, economic, and political center of Uzbekistan.

Geography and Climate

Uzbekistan's geography is characterized by diverse landscapes. The country is predominantly flat, with expansive deserts like the Kyzylkum Desert and the Aral Sea region. The fertile Fergana Valley, surrounded by majestic mountains, is an oasis of agricultural abundance. The Tian Shan and Pamir-Alay mountain ranges offer breathtaking scenery and opportunities for outdoor adventures.

The climate in Uzbekistan is continental, with hot summers and cold winters. In summer, temperatures can soar above 40°C (104°F) in the lowland areas, while winters can be bitterly cold, especially in the mountainous regions. Spring and autumn are considered the most pleasant seasons for visiting, with mild temperatures and comfortable weather.

History and Culture

Uzbekistan, a landlocked country in Central Asia, boasts a rich and diverse history that spans thousands of years. The region served as a vital crossroad on the ancient Silk Road, connecting the East and the West and facilitating trade and cultural exchange. Throughout its history, Uzbekistan has been influenced by various civilizations, each leaving a profound impact on its cultural tapestry.

The Persians, Greeks, Arabs, Mongols, and Timurids are among the many civilizations that have shaped Uzbekistan's history. The legacy of these civilizations can be witnessed in the architectural masterpieces scattered across the country. Uzbekistan is renowned for its magnificent mosques, grand madrasas (Islamic schools), ornate mausoleums, and formidable fortresses. These structures stand as testaments to the country's rich heritage and showcase the finest examples of Islamic architecture and urban planning. The cities of Samarkand, Bukhara, and Khiva, with their UNESCO World Heritage Sites status, are treasure troves of historical and architectural marvels.

Uzbekistan's culture is a vibrant fusion of diverse influences, blending elements from the various civilizations that have called the region home. Traditional arts and crafts, such as pottery, silk weaving, carpet making, and miniature painting, have been passed down through generations, preserving the country's artistic traditions. The Uzbek cuisine is a delightful blend of flavors, with dishes like plov (rice pilaf), shashlik (grilled meat skewers), and manti (dumplings) tantalizing the taste buds of both locals and visitors.

Music, dance, and literature also play integral roles in Uzbek culture. Traditional Uzbek music, characterized by the soulful melodies of the stringed instruments such as the dutar and the tanbur, creates an enchanting ambiance. Dance forms like the lively and colorful "Lazgi" and the graceful "Beshkempir" showcase the country's rich cultural heritage. Uzbek literature, with renowned poets and authors like Alisher Navoi and Abdulla Qodiriy, holds a significant place in the literary world.

The people of Uzbekistan are known for their warm hospitality and strong sense of tradition. Traditional values, such as strong family ties and a deep-rooted sense of community, play a central role in Uzbek society. Visitors to Uzbekistan are often welcomed with open arms and can experience the genuine warmth and kindness of the Uzbek people.

Uzbekistan's journey through history has shaped its cultural identity and transformed it into a captivating destination for travelers seeking a glimpse into the past. With its awe-inspiring historical sites, breathtaking natural landscapes, and vibrant cultural traditions, Uzbekistan offers an unforgettable experience that truly reflects the heart and soul of Central Asia. From exploring the ancient cities to savoring the local cuisine and engaging with the friendly locals, every moment spent in Uzbekistan is a journey through time and a celebration of its rich heritage.

CHAPTER ONE
Getting Ready for Your Trip
Visa Requirements and Entry Formalities

As a world-class tourist, embarking on a journey to Uzbekistan requires careful preparation to ensure a smooth entry into the country. Here is a detailed overview of the visa requirements and entry formalities to help you navigate the process seamlessly.

Visa Requirements

Before traveling to Uzbekistan, it is essential to obtain a valid visa unless you are a citizen of one of the visa-exempt countries. To check if your country is visa-exempt or requires a visa, it is recommended to consult the official website of the Ministry of Foreign Affairs of Uzbekistan or contact the Uzbek embassy or consulate in your home country.

Application Process

To apply for a visa, you will need to complete the necessary paperwork and provide supporting documents. The most common type of visa for tourists is the tourist visa, which allows for a stay of up to 30 days. However, if you plan to stay longer or have specific purposes, such as business or study, you may need to apply for a different type of visa.

The visa application process typically involves the following steps

1. Complete the visa application form accurately and legibly.

2. Prepare a valid passport with a minimum of six months validity beyond the intended departure date.

3. Submit a recent passport-sized photograph as per the specifications outlined by the embassy/consulate.

4. Provide a copy of your travel itinerary, including flight reservations and hotel bookings.

5. Pay the visa application fee, which varies depending on the duration and type of visa.

It is recommended to apply for a visa well in advance of your intended travel date to allow sufficient time for processing. The processing time can vary, so it is advisable to check with the embassy/consulate for the most up-to-date information.

Entry Formalities

Upon arrival in Uzbekistan, you will need to go through immigration and customs procedures. Ensure that you have the following documents readily available:

1. Valid passport: Make sure your passport is valid for at least six months beyond your intended departure date from Uzbekistan.

2. Visa: Present your visa to the immigration officer. They may check its validity, so ensure it is easily accessible.

3. Immigration Form: Fill out the immigration form provided either on the plane or at the immigration counter. The form typically requires basic personal information, including your name, passport details, purpose of visit, and duration of stay.

4. Customs Declaration: Complete a customs declaration form, indicating any valuable items, currency, or goods you are bringing into the country. Be aware of the customs regulations, particularly regarding restricted or prohibited items.

5. Proof of Accommodation: Carry printed copies of your hotel reservations or accommodation details, as you may be asked to provide them as proof of your stay.

6. Travel Insurance: It is advisable to carry travel insurance that covers medical emergencies, trip cancellations, and lost or stolen belongings. Although not mandatory, having travel insurance provides peace of mind during your journey.

7. Currency: Familiarize yourself with the currency regulations and declare any amounts exceeding the allowed limits. It is recommended to carry a mix of cash (in local currency) and internationally accepted credit/debit cards for convenience.

By adhering to these visa requirements and entry formalities, you will ensure a hassle-free arrival and start your exploration of Uzbekistan on the right foot. Remember to keep your travel documents safe throughout your stay and adhere to the local laws and regulations. Enjoy your journey through this remarkable country and create memories that will last a lifetime.

Currency and Banking

Understanding the currency and banking system in Uzbekistan is essential for a seamless travel experience. This section of your travel guide provides important information regarding currency exchange, banking facilities, and payment options within the country.

Currency

The official currency of Uzbekistan is the Uzbekistani Som (UZS). It is advisable to familiarize yourself with the current exchange rate before your trip. The som is available in various denominations, including banknotes and coins. Banknotes are issued in denominations of 1,000, 5,000, 10,000, 20,000, 50,000, and 100,000 som, while coins are available in smaller denominations.

Currency Exchange

To obtain local currency, it is recommended to exchange your foreign currency at official exchange offices, banks, or authorized currency exchange points. These establishments are widely available in major cities and tourist areas. Avoid exchanging money with street vendors or unofficial channels, as they may offer unfavorable rates or counterfeit currency.

It is advisable to carry a mix of cash (preferably in US dollars or Euros) and internationally accepted credit/debit cards. US dollars are widely accepted in major tourist areas and can be used for larger purchases or to exchange for local currency. Ensure that your bills are clean, unmarked, and in good condition, as damaged or torn bills may not be accepted.

Banking Facilities

Uzbekistan has a well-developed banking system with numerous branches and ATMs available in major cities. Banks typically operate from Monday to Friday, with some branches open on Saturdays as well. ATMs are widely accessible, allowing you to withdraw local currency using your international debit or credit card. However, it is advisable to carry sufficient cash, especially when traveling to more remote areas where ATMs may be limited.

Credit/Debit Cards

Credit cards, such as Visa and Mastercard, are accepted in upscale hotels, restaurants, and larger establishments in urban areas. However, it is important to note that cash remains the primary mode of payment in smaller shops, markets, and rural areas. Inform your bank or credit card provider about your travel plans to avoid any issues with card transactions.

Traveler's Checks

While traveler's checks were once a popular option, their usage has declined in recent years, and it may be challenging to find establishments that accept them. It is advisable to rely on cash or cards for most of your transactions.

Currency Regulations

When entering or exiting Uzbekistan, you are required to declare any amount exceeding the equivalent of 5,000 USD in cash or its equivalent in another currency. Ensure that you keep the customs declaration form provided on arrival, as you may be required to present it when leaving the country.

Keep in mind that while larger establishments accept major foreign currencies, it is always recommended to carry local currency for smaller transactions and when venturing outside urban areas.

By understanding the currency and banking system in Uzbekistan, you will be well-prepared to handle your financial needs throughout your journey. Remember to keep your money secure, be mindful of your spending, and have a contingency plan in case of any unforeseen circumstances. Enjoy your time exploring the wonders of Uzbekistan while keeping your financial matters in order.

Language and Communication

When traveling to Uzbekistan, familiarizing yourself with a few basic phrases in the local language can greatly enhance your communication and interactions with the locals. Although Russian is widely spoken and understood, particularly in urban areas, learning a few key phrases in Uzbek will go a long way in connecting with the people and immersing yourself in the local culture. Here are 20 useful phrases to help you navigate your way:

1. Hello - Salom

2. Goodbye - Xayr

3. Thank you - Rahmat

4. Please - Iltimos

5. Yes - Ha

6. No - Yo'q

7. Excuse me - Kechirasiz

8. I'm sorry - Kechirasiz

9. Do you speak English? - Siz ingliz tilini gapirasizmi?

10. I don't understand - Tushunmadim

11. Could you help me, please? - Yordam berishingiz mumkinmi, iltimos?

12. How much does it cost? - Qancha narx?

13. Where is...? - ...qayerda?

14. I would like... - Men ... istar edim.

15. Can I have the menu, please? - Menyuni olishim mumkinmi, iltimos?

16. Cheers! - Tinchlik uchun!

17. Can you recommend a good restaurant? - Yaxshi restoran tavsiya qilasizmi?

18. What time is it? - Soat nechchada?

19. Where is the bathroom? - Hojatxona qayerda?

20. Help! - Yordam!

Remember, locals appreciate the effort when tourists try to communicate in their language. Even if your pronunciation isn't perfect, a genuine attempt will be well received.

Additionally, it is useful to have a translation app or a phrasebook handy to assist with more complex conversations or specific requests. The willingness to engage and communicate will undoubtedly enrich your travel experience and create meaningful connections with the people you encounter along the way.

So, don't hesitate to practice these phrases, greet the locals with a warm "Salom," and embrace the beauty of the Uzbek language as you explore the remarkable country of Uzbekistan.

Transportation in Uzbekistan

Getting to Uzbekistan is an exciting part of your journey, and understanding the transportation options available will help you plan your trip efficiently. Here are some key transportation options to consider when traveling to Uzbekistan:

By Air

The most common and convenient way to reach Uzbekistan is by air. The country has several international airports, with the largest being Tashkent International Airport (TAS). It serves as the main gateway for international flights, connecting Uzbekistan to major cities around the world. Additionally, there are international airports in Samarkand, Bukhara, Urgench (for Khiva), and Navoi.

By Land

If you are traveling from neighboring countries, entering Uzbekistan by land is an option. Uzbekistan shares borders with Kazakhstan, Tajikistan, Kyrgyzstan, Afghanistan, and Turkmenistan. There are border crossings and transport links that allow for overland travel. However, it is advisable to check the current status of border crossings, visa requirements, and transportation availability before planning your journey.

Domestic Flights

Uzbekistan has a well-developed domestic flight network, connecting major cities within the country. Domestic flights are a convenient option if you wish to cover long distances quickly. Uzbekistan Airways, the national carrier, operates domestic flights between Tashkent, Samarkand, Bukhara, Urgench, and other cities. It is recommended to book domestic flights in advance, especially during peak travel seasons.

Train Travel

Train travel in Uzbekistan offers a scenic and culturally immersive experience. The country has an extensive rail network, connecting major cities and towns. The train journey allows you to witness the beautiful landscapes and interact with locals. Tashkent serves as the central hub, offering connections to cities like Samarkand, Bukhara, and Urgench. The trains vary in comfort and speed, with options ranging from regular trains to high-speed trains like the Afrosiyob.

Public Transportation

Once in Uzbekistan, public transportation options such as buses, minibusses (known as marshrutkas), and taxis are available within cities and for intercity travel. Tashkent has an extensive metro system, making it a convenient and affordable way to navigate the city. In other cities, buses and marshrutkas are common modes of transport, offering affordable travel options for shorter distances. Taxis can be hailed on the street or arranged through ride-hailing apps.

Car Rental

Renting a car gives you the flexibility to explore Uzbekistan at your own pace, especially if you plan to visit remote areas or less touristy destinations. Car rental companies can be found in major cities and at airports. It is important to have an international driving permit and familiarize yourself with local driving regulations and road conditions. Keep in mind that traffic rules and driving styles may differ from what you're accustomed to.

Guided Tours and Private Transfers

If you prefer a hassle-free experience, guided tours and private transfers are popular options in Uzbekistan. Local tour operators offer a range of packages that include transportation, accommodation, and guided sightseeing. Private transfers provide the convenience of door-to-door transportation, ensuring a comfortable and tailored experience.

As you plan your journey, consider a combination of transportation modes that best suit your itinerary and travel preferences. Each option offers its own advantages, allowing you to explore the diverse landscapes and cultural treasures of Uzbekistan. Enjoy the journey and embrace the opportunities for adventure and discovery that await you in this enchanting country.

Packing Tips

When preparing for your trip to Uzbekistan, efficient packing ensures a comfortable and enjoyable travel experience. Here are some categorized packing tips to help you organize your essentials effectively:

Clothing

1. Layering: Pack lightweight and breathable clothing that can be layered for varying temperatures. This allows you to adjust to the weather conditions and cultural norms.

2. Modest Attire: Respect local customs by including modest clothing options, especially when visiting religious sites. Carry long-sleeved shirts, pants, and dresses that cover the knees and shoulders.

3. Comfortable Shoes: Uzbekistan's historic cities often require walking on uneven surfaces, so pack comfortable walking shoes or sneakers for sightseeing.

4. Scarf or Shawl: Carry a scarf or shawl, which can serve multiple purposes such as covering your head, shoulders, or providing additional warmth.

Weather Considerations

1. Sun Protection: Pack sunscreen, a hat, and sunglasses to protect yourself from the strong Central Asian sun.

2. Rain Gear: Depending on the season, consider packing a lightweight waterproof jacket or umbrella to prepare for unexpected showers.

3. Winter Essentials: If traveling during winter, include warm clothing such as a coat, gloves, hat, and scarf to combat the cold temperatures, especially in mountainous regions.

Essential Items:

1. Travel Documents: Keep your passport, visa, travel insurance, and other important documents in a secure and easily accessible place.

2. Money and Currency: Carry a mix of cash in Uzbekistani Som (UZS) and internationally accepted debit/credit cards. Ensure your cards are enabled for international use.

3. Electronic Gadgets: Don't forget to pack your camera, mobile phone, chargers, and adapters to capture memories and stay connected.

4. Medications: If you take any prescription medications, bring an adequate supply for the duration of your trip, along with a copy of the prescriptions.

5. Travel Essentials: Include items such as a travel adapter, a universal power bank, a reusable water bottle, and a small first aid kit.

Other Considerations

1. Backpack or Day Bag: Carry a lightweight and durable backpack or day bag to hold your essentials during day trips and city explorations.

2. Toiletries: Pack travel-sized toiletries, including a small towel, hand sanitizer, wet wipes, and any personal care items you require.

3. Language Guide: Consider carrying a phrasebook or language guide to facilitate communication and immerse yourself in the local culture.

It is important to pack smartly and avoid overpacking, as it can restrict your mobility and make it challenging to carry your belongings. Check the weather forecast before your trip and plan your outfits accordingly. Remember to respect local customs and dress appropriately, especially when visiting religious sites.

By following these packing tips, you will be well-prepared for your journey through Uzbekistan. Leave some space in your suitcase for the unique souvenirs you may find along the way, and embrace the adventures that await you in this captivating country. Safe travels!

Accommodation options

Luxury Accommodation

Hyatt Regency Tashkent (Tashkent)

Hyatt Regency Tashkent is a prestigious 5-star hotel located in the heart of Tashkent, the capital city of Uzbekistan. This luxurious hotel provides an exquisite experience for discerning travelers with its elegant accommodations and world-class amenities. Here are the features and facilities offered by Hyatt Regency Tashkent:

Luxurious Rooms and Suites: The hotel offers a range of spacious and tastefully decorated rooms and suites that provide a luxurious and comfortable stay. Guests can expect plush bedding, stylish furnishings, and modern amenities. The rooms are designed to provide a relaxing environment, with large windows offering stunning views of the cityscape.

Dining Options: Hyatt Regency Tashkent boasts a variety of dining options to satisfy every palate. The hotel features multiple restaurants and bars that offer a diverse range of cuisines, from international dishes to local Uzbek specialties. Guests can indulge in fine dining experiences, enjoy casual meals, or relax with a drink at one of the stylish bars.

Spa and Wellness Facilities: The hotel's spa offers a serene oasis where guests can rejuvenate their mind, body, and soul. It features a range of treatments, including massages, facials, and body therapies, provided by skilled therapists. Additionally, there is a sauna, steam room, and a well-equipped fitness center for guests who wish to maintain their exercise routine while traveling.

Swimming Pool: Hyatt Regency Tashkent features a spacious swimming pool, surrounded by comfortable loungers and lush greenery. Guests can take a refreshing dip, relax by the poolside, or enjoy poolside food and beverage service.

Business and Event Facilities: For business travelers, the hotel offers state-of-the-art meeting and conference facilities. These include well-appointed meeting rooms, a ballroom, and advanced audiovisual equipment. The hotel's dedicated events team can assist in organizing successful conferences, seminars, and social events.

Concierge Services and Amenities: Hyatt Regency Tashkent provides excellent concierge services, ensuring that guests have a seamless and memorable stay. Additional amenities include 24-hour room service, laundry services, a gift shop, and a business center.

Hyatt Regency Tashkent offers a luxurious retreat for travelers seeking sophistication, comfort, and convenience in the heart of Tashkent. With its elegant accommodations, world-class dining options, spa and wellness facilities, and business amenities, the hotel provides a memorable experience for both leisure and business travelers alike.

Samarqand Registan Plaza (Samarkand)

Samarqand Registan Plaza is a luxurious hotel located in the heart of Samarkand, just a stone's throw away from the iconic Registan Square. This 5-star hotel offers a blend of modern comfort and traditional Uzbek hospitality, ensuring a memorable stay for its guests. Here are the features and facilities offered by Samarqand Registan Plaza:

Spacious and Well-Appointed Rooms: The hotel provides spacious and well-appointed rooms that exude elegance and comfort. Guests can enjoy tastefully decorated accommodations with modern amenities, including plush bedding, a minibar, a flat-screen TV, and a seating area. The rooms are designed to provide a peaceful retreat after a day of exploring the city.

Rooftop Terrace with Panoramic Views: Samarqand Registan Plaza boasts a rooftop terrace that offers breathtaking panoramic views of the city's historical landmarks, including the majestic Registan Square. Guests can enjoy the stunning sunset or relax in the evening breeze while taking in the mesmerizing beauty of Samarkand's skyline.

Restaurant Serving Uzbek and International Cuisine: The hotel's restaurant offers a diverse culinary experience, featuring both Uzbek and international cuisines. Guests can savor traditional Uzbek dishes, including succulent kebabs, flavorful pilaf, and aromatic soups, as well as indulge in international favorites. The restaurant creates a delightful blend of flavors, catering to various palates.

Fitness Center and Spa: Samarqand Registan Plaza provides a well-equipped fitness center for guests who wish to maintain their fitness routine during their stay. The center offers a range of exercise equipment and facilities for a comprehensive workout experience. Additionally, guests can pamper themselves at the hotel's spa, where skilled therapists offer various treatments and therapies to promote relaxation and rejuvenation.

Conference and Event Facilities: The hotel offers versatile event spaces, including meeting rooms and a ballroom, suitable for business conferences, seminars, and social gatherings. The professional events team at Samarqand Registan Plaza is dedicated to ensuring the success of every event, providing state-of-the-art audiovisual equipment and personalized services.

Concierge Services and Amenities: The hotel's concierge services cater to the needs of its guests, offering assistance with tour arrangements, transportation, and other requests. Additional amenities include 24-hour room service, laundry services, currency exchange, and a gift shop.

Samarqand Registan Plaza offers a luxurious and memorable stay in the enchanting city of Samarkand. With its spacious rooms, rooftop terrace with panoramic views, restaurant serving Uzbek and international cuisine, fitness center, spa, and conference facilities, the hotel provides a perfect blend of comfort, convenience, and cultural immersion for travelers visiting this historical destination.

Asia Bukhara Hotel (Bukhara)

Situated in the heart of Bukhara's Old Town, Asia Bukhara Hotel is an upscale accommodation option that immerses guests in the rich history and charm of this ancient city. This hotel is known for its traditional

Uzbek architecture, warm hospitality, and convenient location. Here are the features and facilities offered by Asia Bukhara Hotel:

Comfortable Rooms: The hotel provides comfortable and well-appointed rooms that are tastefully decorated with traditional Uzbek elements. Guests can enjoy a cozy and relaxing atmosphere, with modern amenities such as air conditioning, flat-screen TVs, minibars, and private bathrooms.

Outdoor Swimming Pool: Asia Bukhara Hotel features an outdoor swimming pool, allowing guests to cool off and unwind in the serene courtyard. The pool is surrounded by loungers and offers a refreshing oasis in the midst of Bukhara's historic setting.

Traditional Uzbek Restaurant: The hotel's restaurant specializes in traditional Uzbek cuisine, offering a delightful culinary experience for guests. Visitors can savor authentic dishes, including flavorful plov (rice pilaf), succulent kebabs, and a variety of regional specialties. The restaurant's cozy ambiance and attentive service add to the overall dining experience.

Cozy Courtyard: Asia Bukhara Hotel's courtyard provides a tranquil space where guests can relax and enjoy the peaceful ambiance. Surrounded by lush greenery, the courtyard offers a serene setting for reading, sipping tea, or simply soaking up the atmosphere of Bukhara's Old Town.

Traditional Uzbek Architecture: The hotel's architecture reflects the traditional Uzbek style, featuring ornate woodwork, intricate tile patterns, and decorative elements that showcase the region's rich cultural heritage. Staying at Asia Bukhara Hotel allows guests to appreciate the authentic Uzbek architectural design and immerse themselves in the historical ambiance of Bukhara.

Warm Hospitality: The staff at Asia Bukhara Hotel is known for their warm hospitality and attentive service. Guests can expect personalized assistance and a friendly atmosphere throughout their stay, ensuring a comfortable and memorable experience.

Asia Bukhara Hotel offers a combination of comfort, traditional charm, and convenient location in the heart of Bukhara's Old Town. With its comfortable rooms, outdoor swimming pool, traditional Uzbek restaurant, cozy courtyard, traditional architecture, and warm hospitality, the hotel provides a delightful haven for travelers seeking a memorable stay in this historic city.

Mid-Range Accommodation
Grand Mir Hotel (Tashkent)

Grand Mir Hotel is a centrally located 4-star hotel in Tashkent, Uzbekistan. With its well-appointed rooms, excellent dining options, fitness facilities, and convenient amenities, it provides a comfortable stay for both business and leisure travelers. Here are the features and facilities offered by Grand Mir Hotel:

Well-Appointed Rooms: The hotel offers well-appointed rooms with modern amenities and comfortable furnishings. Guests can expect spacious accommodations, plush bedding, air conditioning, flat-screen TVs, minibars, and en-suite bathrooms. The rooms are designed to provide a relaxing and enjoyable stay.

Restaurant Serving International Cuisine: Grand Mir Hotel features a restaurant that serves a variety of international cuisines, catering to diverse culinary preferences. Guests can enjoy a range of dishes prepared by skilled chefs, with options for breakfast, lunch, and dinner. The restaurant offers a comfortable and inviting ambiance for a delightful dining experience.

Fitness Center: The hotel provides a fitness center equipped with modern exercise equipment, allowing guests to maintain their fitness routine while traveling. Whether guests prefer cardio workouts or strength training, the fitness center offers a convenient space to stay active during their stay.

Meeting and Conference Facilities: For business travelers, Grand Mir Hotel offers meeting and conference facilities, including well-equipped meeting rooms and a ballroom. These spaces are suitable for hosting various events, such as conferences, seminars, and corporate gatherings. The hotel's professional staff can assist in organizing and planning successful business events.

Concierge Services: The hotel's friendly and attentive staff provides excellent concierge services to assist guests with their needs. Whether it's arranging transportation, recommending local attractions, or providing information about the city, the concierge team is dedicated to ensuring a pleasant and convenient stay for every guest.

Central Location: Grand Mir Hotel enjoys a convenient location in Tashkent, offering easy access to popular attractions, shopping centers, and business districts. Guests can explore the city's cultural sites, visit local markets, or take advantage of the hotel's proximity to transportation hubs for convenient travel.

Grand Mir Hotel is known for its friendly staff, comfortable accommodations, and convenient location. Whether guests are visiting for business or leisure, the hotel provides a pleasant stay with its well-appointed rooms, international restaurant, fitness center, meeting facilities, and attentive service.

Malika Prime Hotel (Samarkand)

Malika Prime Hotel is a charming mid-range hotel located near the iconic Registan Square in Samarkand, Uzbekistan. This hotel offers comfortable accommodations with traditional Uzbek-style décor, a restaurant serving local dishes, a garden terrace, and a friendly atmosphere. Here are the features and facilities offered by Malika Prime Hotel:

Comfortable Rooms: The hotel provides comfortable rooms with a touch of Uzbek-style décor, creating a warm and inviting ambiance. Guests can expect cozy bedding, air conditioning, private bathrooms, and other essential amenities for a pleasant stay. The rooms are designed to reflect the rich cultural heritage of Uzbekistan, combining traditional elements with modern comfort.

Restaurant Offering Local Dishes: Malika Prime Hotel features a restaurant that offers a taste of Uzbek cuisine. Guests can savor local dishes prepared with fresh ingredients and authentic flavors. From hearty plov (rice pilaf) to flavorful shashlik (grilled meat skewers) and savory soups, the restaurant showcases the diverse culinary traditions of Uzbekistan. The attentive staff and cozy atmosphere create an enjoyable dining experience.

Garden Terrace: The hotel's garden terrace provides a tranquil space where guests can relax and unwind. Surrounded by lush greenery and blooming flowers, the terrace offers a peaceful retreat from the bustling city. Guests can enjoy a cup of tea or coffee while soaking up the pleasant atmosphere and enjoying the beautiful views.

Friendly Atmosphere: Malika Prime Hotel is known for its friendly and welcoming atmosphere. The staff members are attentive and go the extra mile to ensure that guests have a comfortable and enjoyable stay. They provide personalized service, assisting guests with any inquiries or requests, and offering recommendations for exploring the city.

Convenient Location: The hotel's proximity to Registan Square makes it an ideal base for exploring the historical treasures of Samarkand. Guests can easily walk to the famous Registan Square and other popular attractions, immersing themselves in the city's rich history and architectural wonders.

Malika Prime Hotel offers a comfortable and authentic experience in the heart of Samarkand. With its comfortable rooms featuring Uzbek-style décor, a restaurant offering local dishes, a garden terrace, and a friendly atmosphere, the hotel provides a pleasant stay for travelers seeking a mid-range option with a touch of local charm.

Amulet Hotel (Bukhara)

Amulet Hotel is a charming accommodation located within the historic old town of Bukhara, Uzbekistan. This hotel offers cozy rooms adorned with traditional Uzbek design, a courtyard café, and a rooftop terrace with panoramic views of Bukhara's enchanting skyline. It is renowned for its authentic atmosphere and helpful staff. Here are the features and facilities offered by Amulet Hotel:

Cozy Rooms with Traditional Uzbek Design: Amulet Hotel provides cozy rooms that showcase the traditional Uzbek design and decor. Guests can expect comfortable bedding, traditional textiles, and intricate woodwork that reflects the rich cultural heritage of Bukhara. The rooms create a warm and welcoming ambiance, immersing guests in the traditional Uzbek atmosphere.

Courtyard Café: The hotel features a charming courtyard café where guests can enjoy a leisurely meal or sip a cup of tea amidst a peaceful setting. The café offers a relaxed and cozy atmosphere, allowing guests to unwind and soak up the authentic Bukhara experience.

Rooftop Terrace with Panoramic Views: Amulet Hotel boasts a rooftop terrace that offers breathtaking panoramic views of Bukhara's historic landmarks and architectural wonders. Guests can enjoy the stunning vistas, especially during sunrise or sunset, capturing the beauty of the city's skyline. The rooftop terrace provides a tranquil space to relax and take in the magical atmosphere of Bukhara.

Authentic Atmosphere: Amulet Hotel is renowned for its authentic atmosphere, providing guests with a true taste of the old-world charm of Bukhara. The hotel's architecture, decor, and attentive service create an ambiance that transports guests back in time, allowing them to immerse themselves in the rich history and culture of the city.

Helpful Staff: The staff at Amulet Hotel is known for their helpful and friendly nature. They are dedicated to ensuring that guests have a comfortable and memorable stay, offering assistance with local recommendations, transportation arrangements, and any other needs that guests may have.

Convenient Location: Amulet Hotel's location within the historic old town of Bukhara provides easy access to the city's main attractions and cultural sites. Guests can explore the ancient mosques, madrasas, and bustling bazaars, all within walking distance from the hotel.

Amulet Hotel offers a unique and authentic experience in the heart of Bukhara. With its cozy rooms featuring traditional Uzbek design, a courtyard café, a rooftop terrace with panoramic views, an authentic atmosphere, and helpful staff, the hotel provides a memorable stay for travelers seeking an intimate and charming accommodation option.

Budget Accommodation
Topchan Hostel (Tashkent)

Topchan Hostel is a budget-friendly accommodation option in Tashkent, Uzbekistan, known for its affordability and comfortable amenities. This hostel is popular among backpackers and budget travelers looking for a cozy and affordable place to stay. Here are the features and facilities offered by Topchan Hostel:

Dormitory-Style Rooms with Shared Facilities: Topchan Hostel offers dormitory-style rooms with bunk beds, providing an affordable accommodation option for solo travelers or groups. Guests share bathroom facilities, which are clean and well-maintained. The hostel provides lockers or storage space to keep personal belongings secure.

Communal Kitchen: The hostel features a communal kitchen where guests can prepare their meals and socialize with fellow travelers. This shared kitchen space is equipped with cooking utensils, a stove, a refrigerator, and dining areas. It allows guests to save money by preparing their own meals and offers an opportunity for cultural exchange.

Cozy Lounge Area: Topchan Hostel provides a cozy lounge area where guests can relax, read a book, or mingle with other travelers. The lounge is furnished with comfortable seating, creating a friendly and inviting atmosphere for guests to unwind and share travel experiences.

Friendly and Helpful Staff: The hostel's staff members are known for their friendly and helpful nature. They are available to assist guests with any inquiries, provide local recommendations, and ensure a pleasant and hassle-free stay. The staff's local knowledge can be valuable in helping guests navigate the city and discover hidden gems.

Affordability and Value: Topchan Hostel offers affordable rates, making it an ideal choice for budget-conscious travelers. Despite its budget-friendly nature, the hostel maintains cleanliness and provides essential amenities to ensure a comfortable stay. Guests can enjoy the convenience and affordability of this accommodation option while exploring Tashkent.

Social Atmosphere: The hostel's communal facilities, including the kitchen and lounge area, encourage social interaction among guests. Travelers have the opportunity to meet people from around the world, share travel experiences, and create lasting friendships. This social atmosphere adds to the overall experience of staying at Topchan Hostel.

Convenient Location: Topchan Hostel is situated in a convenient location within Tashkent, with easy access to public transportation, restaurants, and local attractions. Guests can explore the city's sights, such as museums, markets, and parks, without having to travel far from the hostel.

Topchan Hostel offers a comfortable and affordable stay for budget travelers in Tashkent. With its dormitory-style rooms, shared facilities, communal kitchen, cozy lounge area, friendly staff, affordability, and convenient location, the hostel provides a welcoming and budget-conscious option for those looking to explore Tashkent on a budget.

Meros Guesthouse (Samarkand)

Meros Guesthouse is a budget-friendly accommodation option in Samarkand, Uzbekistan. This guesthouse offers budget rooms with shared bathrooms, a communal kitchen, and a rooftop terrace. It provides a friendly atmosphere and a convenient location near major attractions. Here are the features and facilities offered by Meros Guesthouse:

Budget Rooms with Shared Bathrooms: Meros Guesthouse provides budget rooms that are clean and comfortable, offering a cost-effective accommodation option for travelers on a budget. Guests have access to shared bathrooms, which are well-maintained and equipped with necessary amenities.

Communal Kitchen: The guesthouse features a communal kitchen where guests can prepare their meals and interact with other travelers. The kitchen is equipped with cooking facilities, utensils, and a dining area. It offers a convenient space for guests to cook their own meals, share culinary experiences, and save money on dining expenses.

Rooftop Terrace: Meros Guesthouse offers a rooftop terrace that provides panoramic views of the city. Guests can relax and unwind on the terrace, enjoying the breathtaking vistas of Samarkand's architectural wonders. It serves as a tranquil space to enjoy a cup of tea or coffee while soaking in the city's ambiance.

Friendly Atmosphere: The guesthouse is known for its friendly and welcoming atmosphere. The staff members are helpful and go the extra mile to ensure that guests have a pleasant stay. They provide assistance with local recommendations, transportation arrangements, and any other needs that guests may have.

Convenient Location: Meros Guesthouse is conveniently located near major attractions in Samarkand, allowing guests to explore the city's historical sites and landmarks with ease. Visitors can easily walk to popular attractions such as the Registan Square, Bibi-Khanym Mosque, and Shah-i-Zinda. The guesthouse's central location saves time and transportation costs for guests.

Affordability and Value: Meros Guesthouse offers affordable rates, making it an ideal choice for budget travelers. Despite its budget-friendly nature, the guesthouse maintains cleanliness and provides essential amenities to ensure a comfortable stay. Guests can enjoy the affordability and value offered by Meros Guesthouse while experiencing the charm of Samarkand.

Meros Guesthouse provides budget-conscious travelers with a comfortable and affordable stay in Samarkand. With its budget rooms, shared bathrooms, communal kitchen, rooftop terrace, friendly atmosphere, and convenient location near major attractions, the guesthouse offers a welcoming and cost-effective option for exploring the captivating city of Samarkand.

Old City Hostel (Bukhara)

Old City Hostel is a budget-friendly accommodation located in Bukhara's Old Town, Uzbekistan. This hostel offers dormitory-style rooms, shared facilities, a communal kitchen, and a courtyard, making it a popular choice among budget travelers seeking an affordable and social accommodation option. Here are the features and facilities offered by Old City Hostel:

Dormitory-Style Rooms: Old City Hostel provides dormitory-style rooms with bunk beds, catering to solo travelers or groups on a budget. The rooms are clean and comfortable, offering a budget-friendly option for guests to rest and recharge during their stay. Bedding and lockers are provided for each guest's convenience.

Shared Facilities: The hostel offers shared bathroom facilities, which are well-maintained and hygienic. Guests have access to communal areas, including bathrooms and showers, which are conveniently located for ease of use. The shared facilities ensure affordability and a social atmosphere among guests.

Communal Kitchen: Old City Hostel features a communal kitchen where guests can prepare their meals, interact with other travelers, and share culinary experiences. The kitchen is equipped with cooking utensils, a stove, a refrigerator, and dining areas. It provides an opportunity for budget-conscious travelers to cook their own meals and save money on dining expenses.

Courtyard: The hostel boasts a charming courtyard where guests can relax, socialize, and enjoy the pleasant Bukhara weather. The courtyard offers a tranquil space for guests to unwind, read a book, or have conversations with fellow travelers. It adds to the social atmosphere and provides a cozy outdoor setting within the hostel.

Affordability and Social Atmosphere: Old City Hostel is known for its affordability and social atmosphere, attracting budget travelers from around the world. The communal areas, such as the kitchen and courtyard, encourage interaction among guests, allowing for cultural exchange and the creation of lasting friendships. The hostel's friendly and welcoming environment fosters a sense of community.

Convenient Location: The hostel's location in Bukhara's Old Town offers convenient access to the city's main attractions, including historical sites, markets, and local restaurants. Guests can easily explore the rich heritage of Bukhara on foot, as many popular landmarks are within walking distance from the hostel.

Old City Hostel provides an affordable and social accommodation option in the heart of Bukhara's Old Town. With its dormitory-style rooms, shared facilities, communal kitchen, courtyard, affordability, and convenient location, the hostel offers a budget-friendly and engaging experience for travelers looking to explore Bukhara without breaking the bank.

CHAPTER TWO
Exploring Uzbekistan

Tashkent, the capital city of Uzbekistan, is a vibrant metropolis that seamlessly blends modernity with rich cultural heritage. Explore its bustling streets, admire its architectural wonders, and immerse yourself in the local traditions. This section of your travel guide will take you through the highlights of Tashkent, from must-visit landmarks to dining experiences and entertainment options.

Tashkent City

Located in the northeastern part of Uzbekistan, Tashkent stands as a vibrant and modern city that beautifully showcases the fusion of historical charm and contemporary development. Let's delve deeper into the various aspects that make Tashkent a captivating destination to explore.

Historical Significance

Tashkent has a rich history that dates back over 2,000 years. The city has witnessed the rise and fall of numerous empires, including the Mauryan, Persian, and Mongol empires. Throughout its history, Tashkent served as a significant hub along the ancient Silk Road, facilitating trade and cultural exchange between East and West.

Cosmopolitan Atmosphere

Tashkent embraces its status as a cosmopolitan city, offering a melting pot of cultures and ethnicities. Uzbekistan's capital is home to people from various backgrounds, including Uzbeks, Tajiks, Russians, Koreans, and Tatars. This multicultural blend is reflected in the city's vibrant atmosphere, diverse culinary scene, and the range of languages spoken.

Modern Infrastructure

Tashkent's urban landscape is characterized by modern architecture, wide boulevards, and well-planned infrastructure. The city boasts contemporary amenities such as modern shopping malls, luxury hotels, and international restaurants. The skyline is adorned with towering skyscrapers, adding to the cosmopolitan feel of the city.

Green Spaces and Parks

Tashkent is known for its abundance of green spaces and well-maintained parks. The city takes pride in its commitment to preserving the environment and providing recreational spaces for its residents and visitors. Some popular parks include Alisher Navoi National Park, Independence Park, and Babur Park, which offer peaceful retreats amidst the bustling cityscape.

Cultural Centers and Institutions

Tashkent serves as a hub for cultural activities, housing numerous theaters, museums, and art galleries. The city boasts several renowned institutions, including the State Academic Bolshoi Theatre of Uzbekistan, the State Museum of History of Uzbekistan, and the Navoi Opera and Ballet Theatre. These cultural centers showcase a range of performances, exhibitions, and artistic endeavors, representing the rich cultural heritage of Uzbekistan.

Transportation Hub

With its well-connected transportation network, Tashkent serves as a major transportation hub in Central Asia. The city is served by Tashkent International Airport (TAS), offering flights to and from international destinations. It is also a hub for domestic flights and has a well-developed railway system, connecting Tashkent to other cities within Uzbekistan and neighboring countries.

Economic and Political Center

Tashkent plays a vital role in Uzbekistan's economy and politics. The city houses the headquarters of government institutions, international organizations, and multinational corporations. Its strategic location, well-developed infrastructure, and business-friendly environment make it an attractive destination for commerce and investment.

As you explore Tashkent, you will witness the juxtaposition of its historical roots with its contemporary development. The city's cosmopolitan atmosphere, green spaces, cultural institutions, and modern amenities create a unique blend that captivates the senses and offers a glimpse into the diverse facets of Uzbekistan's capital.

Must-Visit Landmarks and Monuments

Tashkent boasts a rich historical and architectural heritage, with numerous landmarks and monuments that showcase the country's cultural legacy. Some must-visit sites include:

Amir Timur Square

Amir Timur Square is one of the most iconic landmarks in Tashkent, located at the heart of the city. This grand central square pays homage to the great Central Asian conqueror, Amir Timur, also known as Tamerlane. Here's a detailed exploration of this historical square:

Historical Significance

Amir Timur, born in 1336, was a prominent figure in Central Asian history and the founder of the Timurid Empire. He led successful military campaigns and his empire spanned from present-day Iran to India and from the Mediterranean to Siberia. Known for his military prowess and patronage of the arts, Amir Timur left a lasting legacy in the region.

Equestrian Statue of Amir Timur

The centerpiece of Amir Timur Square is the imposing bronze equestrian statue of Amir Timur on horseback. The statue, standing tall at 15 meters (49 feet) high, depicts Amir Timur in his military attire, mounted on a rearing horse. It is a striking representation of his power and leadership.

Architectural Surroundings

The square is surrounded by architecturally impressive buildings that add to its grandeur. The Palaces of Forums, located on the eastern side, stand as a prominent example of Soviet-era architecture. These buildings house various government offices, including the Senate of Uzbekistan.

Floral Arrangements and Fountains

Amir Timur Square is adorned with beautifully landscaped gardens, vibrant flowerbeds, and meticulously designed floral arrangements. The green spaces and colorful blooms create a visually appealing atmosphere, making it a popular spot for locals and tourists alike.

The square also features elegant fountains that enhance its aesthetic appeal. The water elements provide a sense of tranquility and serve as gathering points for people to relax and enjoy the surroundings.

Cultural Significance and Events

Amir Timur Square holds cultural and historical significance for Uzbekistan. It serves as a symbol of national pride, celebrating the country's heritage and achievements. The square has witnessed numerous important events and celebrations, including military parades, cultural festivals, and public gatherings.

Visiting Amir Timur Square

Visitors can explore Amir Timur Square at any time of the day. The square offers ample space for leisurely walks, photography, and appreciating the architectural splendor. The surrounding buildings and the statue of Amir Timur provide excellent backdrops for capturing memorable moments.

The square is particularly enchanting in the evening when the buildings and the statue are illuminated, creating a magical ambiance. The well-maintained gardens and fountains add to the allure, making it an ideal place to unwind and soak in the atmosphere.

Amir Timur Square stands as a testament to the historical legacy of Amir Timur and his significance in Central Asian history. It not only serves as a prominent landmark but also embodies the spirit of Tashkent, celebrating the cultural heritage and achievements of Uzbekistan. A visit to Amir Timur Square offers a glimpse into the country's rich history and a chance to appreciate the grandeur of its architectural treasures.

Independence Square

Independence Square, also known as Mustakillik Square, is a significant landmark in Tashkent that holds great historical and symbolic importance. Spanning across a vast area, the square commemorates Uzbekistan's independence and showcases impressive fountains and monumental structures. Here's a detailed exploration of this remarkable public square:

Historical Significance

Independence Square serves as a powerful symbol of Uzbekistan's sovereignty and independence. It was here, on September 1, 1991, that the Supreme Soviet of the Republic of Uzbekistan declared the country's independence from the Soviet Union. The square stands as a testament to the nation's journey towards self-determination and its commitment to shaping its own destiny.

Monumental Structures

The square is adorned with monumental structures that represent various aspects of Uzbekistan's history and culture. These structures include:

1. Independence Monument

At the center of the square stands the Independence Monument, a towering granite column reaching a height of 80 meters (262 feet). Crowned with a golden statue of a woman holding aloft the national emblem, the monument symbolizes the victory and freedom of Uzbekistan.

2. Monument of Happy Mother

Adjacent to the Independence Monument is the Monument of Happy Mother, dedicated to the courage and strength of Uzbek women. The sculpture portrays a mother joyfully cradling her child, representing the nation's aspirations for a prosperous future.

3. Fountains and Water Features

Independence Square boasts an impressive ensemble of fountains and water features that add to its grandeur. The cascading water creates a serene and visually captivating ambiance. The fountains are carefully designed, featuring intricate patterns and synchronized displays, creating a mesmerizing spectacle for visitors.

Cultural Events and Gatherings

Independence Square serves as a significant venue for cultural events, concerts, and public gatherings. The square has witnessed various national celebrations, festivals, and performances, fostering a sense of unity and patriotism among the Uzbek people.

Visiting Independence Square

Independence Square is open to visitors throughout the day, providing ample space for leisurely walks, relaxation, and photography. The surrounding green spaces and well-manicured gardens offer a tranquil setting amidst the bustling cityscape.

The square is particularly enchanting in the evening when the monuments, fountains, and buildings are beautifully illuminated. The captivating lights and reflections create a magical atmosphere, making it a popular spot for locals and tourists to enjoy the vibrant nightlife of Tashkent.

Surrounding Landmarks

Independence Square is located in the heart of Tashkent, surrounded by notable landmarks and significant buildings. These include the Uzbekistan Hotel, the Palace of International Forums, and the Senate of

Uzbekistan. The proximity to these architectural gems adds to the appeal of visiting the square.

A visit to Independence Square offers a profound insight into Uzbekistan's history, struggle for independence, and the spirit of its people. It is a place where the past and present converge, embodying the nation's journey towards self-determination and progress. The grandeur of the square, combined with its symbolic significance, creates a memorable experience for visitors, leaving a lasting impression of Uzbekistan's rich cultural heritage and national pride.

Khast Imam Square

Khast Imam Square is a spiritual and cultural complex located in the heart of Tashkent, Uzbekistan. This historic square encompasses several significant Islamic institutions and serves as a center for religious and cultural activities. At the heart of the complex lies the Khast Imam Mosque and the Muyi Muborak Library, which houses the world's oldest Quran. Here's a detailed exploration of this remarkable square:

Khast Imam Mosque

The Khast Imam Mosque, also known as the Barak Khan Madrasah, stands as the central feature of the complex. This architectural gem showcases stunning turquoise domes, intricate tilework, and ornate facades. The mosque dates back to the 16th century and underwent extensive restoration in recent years to preserve its historical grandeur.

Muyi Muborak Library

Situated within the Khast Imam Square, the Muyi Muborak Library is a treasure trove of Islamic manuscripts and artifacts. It houses a vast collection of rare religious texts, including the world's oldest Quran, believed to have been written during the 7th century. The library's collection also includes ancient manuscripts, illuminated Qurans, and other valuable Islamic texts.

Islamic Institutions

The Khast Imam Square is home to several significant Islamic institutions that contribute to Uzbekistan's religious and cultural heritage. These institutions include:

1. Tilla Sheikh Mosque: Located adjacent to the Khast Imam Mosque, this historic mosque features a stunning golden dome and intricate blue tilework. It is considered a revered pilgrimage site for Muslims in Uzbekistan.

2. Namazgoh Mosque: Situated within the square, this mosque is known for its beautiful architecture and peaceful ambiance. It provides a place for prayer and reflection for visitors and locals alike.

3. Imam al-Bukhari Islamic Institute: This prestigious institute offers Islamic education and training for scholars and religious leaders. It plays a vital role in preserving and promoting Islamic knowledge in Uzbekistan.

Cultural and Spiritual Significance:

Khast Imam Square holds immense cultural and spiritual significance for Uzbekistan and the wider Islamic world. It serves as a hub for religious activities, including daily prayers, religious ceremonies, and gatherings. The square attracts pilgrims, scholars, and tourists who seek to explore the rich Islamic heritage and experience the spiritual atmosphere.

Visiting Khast Imam Square

Visitors can explore Khast Imam Square to appreciate its architectural beauty and immerse themselves in its spiritual ambiance. The peaceful courtyards and shaded walkways provide a serene environment for contemplation and relaxation. The square is open to visitors throughout the day, allowing ample time to explore the mosque, library, and other surrounding structures.

It is advisable to dress modestly and respectfully when visiting Khast Imam Square, as it is a place of worship and religious significance.

Women should cover their heads and shoulders, and both men and women should ensure their clothing covers their knees.

A visit to Khast Imam Square offers a unique opportunity to witness the preservation of Islamic heritage, explore ancient religious texts, and experience the profound spiritual atmosphere. It is a testament to the cultural richness and religious devotion of Uzbekistan, making it a must-visit destination for travelers seeking a deeper understanding of the country's Islamic heritage.

Chorsu Bazaar

Chorsu Bazaar is a bustling traditional market located in the heart of Tashkent, Uzbekistan. Known for its vibrant atmosphere, rich history, and diverse array of goods, the bazaar offers a unique shopping experience. Here's a detailed exploration of this vibrant marketplace:

Historical Significance

Chorsu Bazaar has a long history dating back to the 9th century when it served as a trading hub along the ancient Silk Road. Over the centuries, it has been a vital center for commerce, connecting traders from various parts of the world. The bazaar has witnessed the exchange of goods, ideas, and cultures, making it an important cultural and historical landmark.

Layout and Architecture

The bazaar's distinctive feature is its domed structure, which has become an iconic symbol of Tashkent. The large blue dome, adorned with intricate tilework, stands tall and is visible from a distance. It houses the main section of the bazaar, creating a unique and captivating architectural sight.

Vibrant Atmosphere

Stepping into Chorsu Bazaar immerses you in a lively and vibrant atmosphere. The air is filled with the aroma of spices, the sounds of vendors calling out their wares, and the vibrant colors of various goods on display. The bazaar is a true feast for the senses, offering an authentic glimpse into the local culture and daily life.

Fresh Produce and Spices

One of the highlights of Chorsu Bazaar is its extensive selection of fresh fruits, vegetables, herbs, and spices. Rows of vibrant stalls are adorned with piles of luscious produce, including succulent melons, juicy pomegranates, and fragrant herbs. It is a haven for food enthusiasts and those seeking to taste the flavors of Uzbekistan.

Handicrafts and Souvenirs

Beyond the realm of food, Chorsu Bazaar offers a wide range of handicrafts, textiles, and souvenirs. Skilled artisans display their craftsmanship, showcasing intricate embroidered fabrics, hand-painted ceramics, traditional Uzbek hats (called tubeteika), and ornate jewelry. These unique and locally made items make perfect souvenirs or gifts to take home.

Local Cuisine and Delicacies

Within Chorsu Bazaar, you'll find small eateries and food stalls offering an array of traditional Uzbek delicacies. Indulge in freshly baked bread, sizzling kebabs, flavorful pilaf (plov), and steaming bowls of hearty soups. It's an excellent opportunity to sample authentic Uzbek cuisine and experience the flavors of the region.

Engaging with Vendors

Interacting with the friendly and welcoming vendors is an integral part of the Chorsu Bazaar experience. Engage in conversations, learn about the products, and embrace the lively exchange that takes place. Many vendors are happy to share their knowledge of local traditions, culinary tips, and stories about the market's history.

Visiting Chorsu Bazaar

Chorsu Bazaar is open daily and is a vibrant hub of activity. It is advisable to visit in the morning to witness the market at its liveliest, with an abundance of fresh produce and enthusiastic vendors. The market can get crowded, so be prepared for a bustling and energetic atmosphere.

As you navigate through Chorsu Bazaar, take your time to explore its nooks and crannies, sample the local flavors, and engage with the vendors. The bazaar offers a unique opportunity to connect with Uzbek culture, savor the richness of its culinary heritage, and find treasures to commemorate your journey through the vibrant marketplace of Tashkent.

Tashkent Metro

Tashkent Metro is an integral part of the city's transportation system and a remarkable architectural gem. Known for its stunning design and intricate artwork, the metro stations offer a unique and visually captivating experience. Here's a detailed exploration of Tashkent Metro and its architectural charm:

Historical Significance

The Tashkent Metro, inaugurated in 1977, holds historical significance as the first underground railway system in Central Asia. It was initially built to serve as a symbol of progress and modernity during the Soviet era, showcasing the technological advancements of that time.

Architectural Splendor

The metro stations of Tashkent are renowned for their architectural charm and attention to detail. Each station has its own unique design, often featuring grand entrances, spacious halls, and intricate decorations.

Artwork and Decorations

One of the highlights of the Tashkent Metro is the extensive artwork and decorations found throughout the stations. The walls are adorned with mosaics, intricate telework, and ornate plasterwork, depicting various themes such as historical events, nature, and cultural symbols.

Chandeliers and Lighting

Another prominent feature of the metro stations is the grand chandeliers that hang from the ceilings, casting a warm glow and adding to the overall ambiance. The lighting design within the stations is carefully crafted to enhance the architectural features and create a visually pleasing environment.

Symbolism and Cultural References

Many of the metro stations in Tashkent have names that reflect historical or cultural significance. For example, Pakhtakor station is named after the famous Pakhtakor Football Club, while Kosmonavtlar station pays tribute to the achievements of Soviet cosmonauts. These names serve as reminders of the city's history and cultural heritage.

Efficiency and Connectivity

Apart from their architectural beauty, Tashkent Metro stations provide efficient transportation services, connecting various parts of the city. The metro system consists of three lines: Chilonzor Line (Line 1), Uzbekistan Line (Line 2), and Yunusabad Line (Line 3). The stations are strategically located, making it convenient for both locals and visitors to navigate Tashkent.

Preservation and Restoration

Over the years, efforts have been made to preserve and restore the original beauty of the Tashkent Metro stations. Restoration projects have aimed to maintain the architectural integrity and artistic value of the stations, ensuring they continue to impress visitors with their timeless appeal.

Exploring the Tashkent Metro

Visitors to Tashkent are encouraged to take a journey on the metro to appreciate the architectural and artistic wonders of its stations. As you descend underground, you'll be transported into a world of captivating designs and cultural references. Take your time to explore each station, admire the artwork, and capture the beauty with your camera.

Please note that photography restrictions may apply in certain areas of the metro stations, so it's essential to respect any guidelines or instructions provided.

Traveling through the Tashkent Metro not only provides efficient transportation but also offers a unique glimpse into the architectural heritage and artistic legacy of the city. It's an experience that showcases the cultural richness and aesthetic appeal of Tashkent, making it an unmissable part of any visit to the capital of Uzbekistan.

State Museum Uzbekistan

The State Museum of History of Uzbekistan, located in Tashkent, offers a captivating journey through the rich history and cultural heritage of Uzbekistan. With its vast collection of artifacts, archaeological finds, and engaging exhibits, the museum provides a comprehensive overview of the region's past. Here's a detailed exploration of the State Museum of History of Uzbekistan:

Architectural Significance

The museum building itself is a work of art, combining elements of traditional Uzbek architecture with modern design. Its grand entrance and spacious halls create an inviting atmosphere, setting the stage for an immersive historical experience.

Collections and Exhibits

The museum boasts an extensive collection that spans various periods of Uzbekistan's history, from ancient civilizations to the modern era. The exhibits are thoughtfully curated, taking visitors on a chronological journey through time.

Archaeological Artifacts

One of the highlights of the museum is its collection of archaeological artifacts, which offers insights into the region's ancient civilizations. Visitors can marvel at ancient pottery, tools, and jewelry, discovering the craftsmanship and artistic achievements of the past.

Art and Craftwork

The museum's exhibits also showcase the artistic and craft traditions of Uzbekistan. Intricately woven carpets, beautifully embroidered textiles, and exquisite metalwork highlight the mastery of Uzbek artisans throughout the ages. These pieces provide a glimpse into the cultural richness and creativity of the region.

Historical Exhibitions

The museum's exhibitions cover significant historical periods, such as the pre-Islamic era, the Silk Road, the Timurid Empire, and the Soviet era. Each exhibition offers a deeper understanding of the political, social, and cultural developments that shaped Uzbekistan's history.

Interactive Displays

To engage visitors further, the museum incorporates interactive displays, multimedia presentations, and immersive experiences. These interactive elements allow visitors to dive deeper into specific historical periods, exploring artifacts and stories in a more engaging and hands-on manner.

Ancient Scripts and Literature

The museum is also home to a remarkable collection of ancient scripts and literature. Visitors can marvel at beautifully preserved manuscripts, including rare Qurans and other religious texts. These artifacts provide a glimpse into the intellectual and literary contributions of Uzbekistan throughout history.

Educational Programs and Events

The museum offers educational programs, guided tours, and lectures to enhance visitors' understanding of Uzbekistan's history. Additionally, it hosts cultural events, temporary exhibitions, and workshops, promoting a deeper appreciation for the country's cultural heritage.

Preserving Cultural Heritage:

The State Museum of History of Uzbekistan plays a crucial role in preserving the country's cultural heritage. Through its conservation efforts, research initiatives, and collaborations with international organizations, the museum contributes to the protection and promotion of Uzbekistan's historical legacy.

Visiting the Museum

The State Museum of History of Uzbekistan welcomes visitors of all ages and backgrounds. It is advisable to allocate sufficient time to explore the exhibits thoroughly and take advantage of any guided tours or educational programs offered. The museum's knowledgeable staff is readily available to provide insights and answer questions, enhancing the overall experience.

A visit to the State Museum of History of Uzbekistan offers a fascinating glimpse into the country's rich and diverse past. From ancient civilizations to the modern era, the museum presents a comprehensive narrative of Uzbekistan's history, preserving its cultural heritage for generations to come. Whether you are a history enthusiast, a cultural explorer, or simply curious about the region's past, the museum promises an enlightening and memorable experience.

State Museum of Applied Arts

The State Museum of Applied Arts in Tashkent is a treasure trove of traditional Uzbek crafts, offering visitors a remarkable collection of artistic creations. The museum showcases a wide range of art forms, including ceramics, textiles, woodwork, metalwork, and jewelry. Here's a detailed exploration of the State Museum of Applied Arts:

Architectural Beauty

The museum is housed in a beautifully restored traditional Uzbek mansion, known as the Usto (Master) Shirin Muradov's House. The building itself is a masterpiece, featuring intricately carved wooden columns, vibrant ceramic tilework, and decorative elements that reflect the architectural style of the region. Its exquisite design sets the stage for the artistic wonders that await inside.

Ceramics and Pottery

One of the museum's prominent collections is its array of ceramics and pottery. Visitors can admire finely crafted vessels, plates, bowls, and decorative objects that showcase the mastery of Uzbek potters. The intricate designs, vibrant colors, and delicate patterns highlight the artistic traditions that have been passed down through generations.

Textiles and Embroidery

The museum also houses a captivating collection of textiles and embroidery, displaying the skill and creativity of Uzbek weavers and embroiderers. Visitors can marvel at the richly woven ikat fabrics, exquisite suzani embroideries, and intricately patterned silk fabrics. These textiles offer insights into the traditional craftsmanship and cultural symbolism that permeate Uzbek culture.

Woodwork and Carvings

Woodwork is another notable art form represented in the museum. Elaborately carved wooden doors, intricately designed furniture, and decorative wooden objects demonstrate the mastery of Uzbek wood craftsmen. The meticulous attention to detail and the combination of traditional motifs create pieces of remarkable beauty and craftsmanship.

Metalwork and Jewelry

The museum's collection of metalwork and jewelry showcases the intricate metal craftsmanship of Uzbek artisans. Visitors can admire finely crafted silver and gold jewelry, ornate belts, traditional headdresses, and decorative metal objects. These pieces reflect the rich heritage of Uzbek jewelry-making, with their exquisite designs and intricate filigree work.

Temporary Exhibitions and Contemporary Crafts

In addition to its permanent collections, the museum often hosts temporary exhibitions that highlight specific themes or showcase contemporary crafts. These exhibitions provide a platform for contemporary artists and artisans to showcase their work and contribute to the preservation and evolution of Uzbek artistic traditions.

Visiting the Museum

When visiting the State Museum of Applied Arts, it is advisable to allocate sufficient time to explore the collections thoroughly. The museum offers guided tours, providing valuable insights into the exhibited artworks and their cultural significance. The knowledgeable staff is available to answer questions and provide further information.

The museum also has a gift shop where visitors can purchase unique handicrafts, textiles, and jewelry, supporting local artisans and taking home a piece of Uzbek cultural heritage.

Navoi Opera and Ballet Theatre

The Navoi Opera and Ballet Theatre in Tashkent is a renowned cultural institution that offers world-class performances of opera and ballet. The theater, named after the renowned Uzbek poet and writer Alisher Navoi, is not only recognized for its artistic excellence but also for its stunning architecture. Here's a detailed exploration of the Navoi Opera and Ballet Theatre:

Architectural Grandeur

The Navoi Theatre is a magnificent architectural masterpiece that reflects the grandeur of its performances. The building features a neoclassical design with majestic columns, a grand entrance, and an impressive facade adorned with sculptures and decorative elements. The theater's exterior alone is a sight to behold and sets the stage for the artistic wonders that await inside.

Artistic Excellence

The theater is home to world-class opera and ballet performances, showcasing the talents of Uzbek and international artists. Audiences can immerse themselves in the enchanting melodies and emotive storytelling of opera or be mesmerized by the graceful movements and exquisite choreography of ballet. The Navoi Theatre is known for its commitment to artistic excellence, ensuring memorable and captivating performances.

The theater offers a diverse repertoire, featuring both classic and contemporary productions. Opera performances include works by renowned composers such as Verdi, Puccini, and Tchaikovsky, while ballet productions feature timeless classics like Swan Lake, Romeo and Juliet, and The Nutcracker. The theater also embraces modern and experimental productions, pushing artistic boundaries and providing a platform for innovation.

Stepping into the Navoi Theatre's interiors is like entering a world of opulence and beauty. The theater hall is adorned with elegant chandeliers, plush seating, and decorative elements that create a luxurious ambiance. The acoustics are meticulously designed to ensure an immersive and exceptional auditory experience for the audience.

Cultural Experience

Attending a performance at the Navoi Opera and Ballet Theatre offers more than just a visual and auditory feast. It is an opportunity to immerse yourself in Uzbek culture, witness the country's artistic talent, and appreciate the deep-rooted appreciation for performing arts in the region. The theater serves as a cultural hub, bringing together local and international artists and fostering a love for opera and ballet among the Uzbek audience.

Ticket Information

Tickets for performances at the Navoi Theatre can be purchased in advance or on the day of the show, subject to availability. It is advisable to check the theater's schedule and book tickets in advance, particularly for popular productions. The theater offers various seating options, accommodating different budget ranges.

Attending a performance at the Navoi Opera and Ballet Theatre is an unforgettable experience that combines artistic excellence, architectural splendor, and cultural immersion. Whether you are a seasoned opera enthusiast or simply curious about experiencing the beauty of ballet, the theater promises an enchanting evening filled with captivating performances and a glimpse into the rich cultural heritage of Uzbekistan.

Shopping and Souvenirs

Tashkent provides ample opportunities for shopping and acquiring unique souvenirs. Some popular shopping destinations include:

Alayskiy Bazaar

Alayskiy Bazaar is a bustling traditional market located in Tashkent, Uzbekistan, offering a vibrant and authentic shopping experience. This market is a popular destination for locals and tourists alike, known for its diverse array of goods and lively atmosphere. Here's a detailed exploration of Alayskiy Bazaar:

Textiles and Clothing

One of the highlights of Alayskiy Bazaar is its wide selection of textiles and clothing. Visitors can find beautifully woven fabrics, colorful traditional Uzbek garments, and intricate embroidery. From silk scarves and ikat fabrics to traditional robes and hats, the market is a treasure trove for those seeking unique and traditional clothing items.

Spices and Culinary Delights

Alayskiy Bazaar is a haven for food enthusiasts. The market offers a rich variety of spices, dried fruits, nuts, and local delicacies. Aromatic spices like cumin, paprika, and saffron can be found, allowing visitors to bring the flavors of Uzbekistan back home. The market is also a great place to sample traditional snacks and sweets, offering a delightful culinary experience.

Traditional Handicrafts

Uzbekistan is renowned for its traditional handicrafts, and Alayskiy Bazaar provides an excellent opportunity to explore these artistic creations. Visitors can browse through a wide range of handicrafts, including hand-painted ceramics, beautifully crafted wooden items, intricate metalwork, and embroidered textiles. These unique and locally made handicrafts make perfect souvenirs or gifts.

Local Produce and Fresh Food

Alayskiy Bazaar is not only a place for shopping but also a vibrant market for fresh produce. Visitors can explore the colorful displays of fruits, vegetables, herbs, and locally sourced products. The market offers a direct connection to the agricultural traditions of Uzbekistan, allowing visitors to experience the flavors of the region and support local farmers.

Chorsu Handicraft Market

Chorsu Handicraft Market is a captivating destination for those seeking traditional Uzbek handicrafts and local artwork. Located near the iconic Chorsu Bazaar in Tashkent, this market showcases the rich cultural heritage of the country. Here's a detailed exploration of Chorsu Handicraft Market:

Embroidered Textiles

Chorsu Handicraft Market is renowned for its exquisite embroidered textiles. Visitors can find beautifully crafted Suzani embroideries, featuring intricate patterns and vibrant colors. These textiles often depict traditional motifs and are representative of the region's rich artistic traditions.

Ceramics and Pottery:

The market offers a diverse selection of ceramics and pottery, ranging from delicate hand-painted tiles to intricately designed vessels and decorative objects. Visitors can explore the artistic mastery of Uzbek potters, appreciating the vibrant colors and unique designs that adorn the ceramics.

Carpets and Rugs

Chorsu Handicraft Market is an excellent place to discover traditional Uzbek carpets and rugs. These handwoven treasures showcase intricate patterns, rich colors, and exceptional craftsmanship. Whether you're looking for a small rug or a large carpet, the market provides a variety of options to suit different tastes.

Miniature Paintings

Uzbekistan is known for its miniature paintings, and Chorsu Handicraft Market is an ideal place to explore this traditional art form. Visitors can find intricately painted miniatures depicting scenes from folklore, history, and everyday life. These miniature paintings make unique and cherished souvenirs.

Jewelry and Accessories

Chorsu Handicraft Market also offers a selection of traditional Uzbek jewelry and accessories. Visitors can browse through beautifully crafted silver and gold jewelry, including earrings, necklaces, bracelets, and traditional headdresses. These pieces reflect the rich heritage of Uzbek jewelry-making, combining intricate designs with cultural symbolism.

Mega Planet Mall and Samarqand Darvoza

For those seeking a modern shopping experience with international brands, electronics, and entertainment options, Tashkent offers Mega Planet Mall and Samarqand Darvoza. These modern shopping centers provide a contrast to the traditional markets and cater to the needs and preferences of contemporary shoppers. Here's a detailed exploration of these shopping destinations:

Mega Planet Mall

Mega Planet Mall is a modern shopping complex in Tashkent, offering a wide range of international and local brands. Visitors can explore a diverse selection of clothing, accessories, electronics, cosmetics, and household goods. The mall provides a comfortable and convenient shopping environment, with spacious walkways, modern amenities, and **a variety of dining options.**

Samarqand Darvoza

Samarqand Darvoza is another modern shopping center in Tashkent, inspired by the rich architectural heritage of the city of Samarkand. This shopping destination combines contemporary retail spaces with traditional design elements, creating a unique and visually appealing environment. Visitors can find a mix of international brands, electronic stores, food courts, and entertainment options.

Entertainment and Leisure

Both Mega Planet Mall and Samarqand Darvoza offer entertainment and leisure options alongside shopping. Visitors can enjoy a movie at the cinema, relax in a cafe or restaurant, or engage in recreational activities such as bowling or gaming. These modern shopping centers provide a space for relaxation, socializing, and entertainment, catering to diverse interests.

Visiting the Markets and Shopping Centers

When visiting Alayskiy Bazaar, Chorsu Handicraft Market, Mega Planet Mall, or Samarqand Darvoza, it's advisable to allocate sufficient time to explore the offerings and take advantage of the unique shopping experiences. The markets and shopping centers have varying opening hours, so it's advisable to check in advance. Remember to negotiate prices when shopping at the traditional markets and be prepared for a lively and vibrant atmosphere.

Whether you're seeking traditional crafts, culinary delights, international brands, or modern entertainment, Tashkent offers a diverse range of shopping experiences to cater to every taste and preference. From exploring the traditional markets to embracing the convenience of modern shopping centers, visitors can indulge in a shopping journey that reflects the cultural diversity and evolving trends of Uzbekistan.

Dining and Local Cuisine

Indulge in the flavors of Uzbek cuisine by exploring Tashkent's diverse dining scene. Some local dishes to savor include:

Plov

Try Plov, Uzbekistan's national dish, is a culinary masterpiece that showcases the rich flavors and cultural heritage of the country. This aromatic rice pilaf is prepared with a combination of meat, carrots, onions, and a blend of aromatic spices, creating a truly memorable dining experience. Here's a detailed exploration of Plov:

The preparation of Plov involves a careful balance of ingredients and cooking techniques that have been passed down through generations. The dish typically starts with sautéing meat, often lamb or beef, in a large pot or cauldron called a kazan. The meat is then cooked until tender and golden brown, infusing the rice with its rich flavors.

One of the defining characteristics of Plov is the blend of aromatic spices that adds depth and complexity to the dish. Common spices used in Plov include cumin, coriander, turmeric, paprika, and black pepper.

These spices create a harmonious blend of flavors, enhancing the overall taste and aroma of the dish.

Plov is known for its perfectly cooked, fluffy rice and tender, succulent pieces of meat. The rice is added to the pot along with the sautéed meat, allowing it to absorb the flavors of the meat and spices. The rice is carefully cooked, ensuring that each grain remains separate and has a delightful texture. The meat becomes tender and juicy, making every bite a delight.

Carrots and onions are integral components of Plov, adding both flavor and vibrant colors to the dish. The carrots are often sliced into thin strips or grated, providing a slightly sweet and earthy taste. The onions are caramelized to bring out their natural sweetness and add a hint of richness to the overall flavor profile.

While Plov is a beloved national dish, there are also regional variations that highlight the culinary diversity of Uzbekistan. For example, in Bukhara, a city in Uzbekistan known for its culinary traditions, Plov may include additional ingredients such as dried fruits, nuts, and spices like saffron. These regional variations add their own unique twists to the classic dish, making each preparation a culinary adventure.

Plov holds great social and cultural significance in Uzbekistan. It is often prepared for festive occasions, weddings, and family gatherings, where it serves as a centerpiece of the meal. The communal act of cooking and sharing Plov brings people together, fostering a sense of unity and celebration.

To experience the authentic flavors of Plov, visitors can seek out local restaurants, cafes, or even street vendors in Uzbekistan. Many eateries specialize in preparing this traditional dish, offering variations to suit different preferences and dietary restrictions. Exploring the local dining scene provides an opportunity to savor Plov in its truest form, prepared by skilled cooks who have mastered the art of this cherished dish.

Plov is more than just a culinary delight; it represents the heart and soul of Uzbek cuisine. Its tantalizing aromas, flavorful rice, and tender meat create an unforgettable dining experience. Trying Plov is a must for any visitor to Uzbekistan, allowing you to connect with the country's rich culinary heritage and indulge in a dish that has stood the test of time.

Shashlik

Shashlik, a popular dish in Uzbekistan, is a delectable culinary delight that showcases the art of grilling and the rich flavors of marinated meat. It consists of skewered and grilled pieces of meat, typically lamb or beef, served with fresh bread and accompanied by savory sauces and salads. Here's a detailed exploration of Shashlik:

Shashlik holds a special place in Uzbek cuisine and culture, as grilling is a cherished culinary tradition in the region. The preparation of Shashlik involves marinating the meat with a blend of spices and flavors, skewering it on long metal or wooden skewers, and grilling it over an open fire. This cooking method imparts a smoky and charred flavor to the meat, creating a succulent and aromatic dish.

Lamb and beef are the most commonly used meats for Shashlik, with each providing its distinct flavor profile. The meat is carefully selected, ensuring the highest quality and tenderness. The marinade is a crucial component of Shashlik, as it adds flavor and tenderizes the meat. The marinade may include ingredients such as onions, garlic, lemon juice, vinegar, and a blend of aromatic spices like cumin, paprika, and black pepper.

The skewered meat is placed on a grill and cooked over an open fire, allowing the heat to infuse the meat with smoky flavors and creating a caramelized exterior. The grilling process requires skill and attention to achieve the perfect balance between a charred exterior and a juicy, tender interior. The meat is turned and basted with marinade during the cooking process, ensuring even cooking and maximum flavor.

Shashlik is traditionally served with fresh bread, such as traditional Uzbek flatbread called "lepyoshka." The bread acts as a vehicle for savoring the succulent pieces of grilled meat. Additionally, Shashlik is often accompanied by savory sauces, such as tomato-based or yogurt-based sauces, which complement the flavors of the meat. Fresh salads, pickles, and sliced onions are also common accompaniments, adding a refreshing and tangy element to the meal.

Shashlik is more than just a dish; it is a social and culinary experience. In Uzbekistan, Shashlik is often enjoyed in a communal setting, where family and friends gather around a grill to cook and share the meal together. This shared experience fosters a sense of togetherness, celebrating the joys of food, conversation, and connection.

Where to Enjoy Shashlik:

To experience the true essence of Shashlik, visitors can explore local restaurants, outdoor markets, or even street food stalls in Uzbekistan. These establishments often specialize in grilling and offer Shashlik as a highlight of their menu. The aroma of sizzling meat and the lively atmosphere of these venues create an authentic and memorable dining experience.

Shashlik represents the art of grilling and the culinary traditions of Uzbekistan. Its tender and flavorful meat, enhanced by the marinade and the grilling process, offers a gastronomic journey that delights the senses. Trying Shashlik in Uzbekistan provides an opportunity to immerse yourself in the vibrant culinary culture of the country, savoring the flavors, and embracing the communal spirit that surrounds this beloved dish.

Samsa

Samsa, a beloved pastry in Uzbek cuisine, is a delightful treat that combines flaky pastry with a savory filling. These baked pastries are typically filled with meat, potatoes, or vegetables, making them a perfect option for a quick snack or a light meal. Here's a detailed exploration of Samsa:

The key to a delicious Samsa lies in its pastry. The pastry dough is made from flour, water, and oil, resulting in a flaky and buttery texture. The dough is carefully prepared and rolled out into thin sheets, which are then folded around the filling, creating a pocket of delectable goodness. The pastry is skillfully baked to achieve a golden and crispy exterior.

Samsa offers a variety of fillings to cater to different tastes and preferences. The most common filling is a combination of minced meat, onions, and fragrant spices such as cumin, coriander, and black pepper. The meat filling provides a rich and savory taste that blends perfectly with the flaky pastry. Additionally, vegetarian options are available, with fillings that include potatoes, carrots, and onions, seasoned with herbs and spices.

The spices used in Samsa play a significant role in enhancing the flavor of the filling. Traditional Uzbek spices, such as cumin, paprika, and coriander, infuse the filling with aromatic notes and a hint of warmth. These spices add depth and complexity to the overall taste of the pastry, tantalizing the taste buds with every bite.

Baking Technique

Samsa is baked in special tandoor ovens, which contribute to the unique texture and flavor of the pastry. The tandoor oven, traditionally made of clay or stone, provides even heat distribution, resulting in a crispy exterior and a moist and flavorful interior. The baking process allows the pastry to develop a golden brown color and a tantalizing aroma.

Samsa is a versatile pastry that can be enjoyed as a quick snack or as a light meal. In Uzbekistan, it is commonly consumed for breakfast, lunch, or as a satisfying snack throughout the day. The portable nature of Samsa makes it a convenient option for on-the-go eating, allowing locals and visitors to indulge in a delicious pastry wherever they may be.

Local Variations

While Samsa is a staple in Uzbek cuisine, there are also regional variations that reflect the diversity of the country's culinary traditions. For example, in Tashkent, the capital city of Uzbekistan, Samsa may be larger in size and feature a spicier filling. In other regions, such as Bukhara or Samarkand, different herbs, spices, or even unique fillings may be used, showcasing the distinct flavors of each locality.

Where to Enjoy Samsa

To experience the authentic taste of Samsa, visitors can explore local bakeries, street food stalls, or even specialty Samsa shops in Uzbekistan. These establishments often have tandoor ovens on-site, baking fresh pastries throughout the day. The aroma of freshly baked Samsa and the sight of locals enjoying this beloved pastry create an enticing and authentic culinary experience.

Samsa offers a delightful blend of flavors and textures, combining flaky pastry with savory fillings. Whether enjoyed as a quick snack or a light meal, Samsa embodies the essence of Uzbek cuisine and is a testament to the country's culinary heritage. Trying Samsa in Uzbekistan allows you to immerse yourself in the local culinary culture, savoring the craftsmanship of the pastry and the satisfying flavors that make it a beloved treat.

Tashkent offers a range of dining options, from cozy local teahouses and traditional Uzbek restaurants to international cuisine and trendy cafes.

Nightlife and Entertainment

Tashkent's nightlife scene offers a mix of entertainment options to suit various preferences. Enjoy live music, dance performances, and traditional Uzbek music concerts at venues like:

Ilkhom Theatre

Ilkhom Theatre is a prominent cultural institution in Tashkent, offering a unique and innovative approach to theater. This contemporary theater showcases a range of performances, including experimental plays, music, and dance, providing a platform for artistic expression and creative exploration. Here's a detailed exploration of Ilkhom Theatre:

Ilkhom Theatre is known for its bold and experimental approach to theater. The performances challenge traditional boundaries and push artistic boundaries, offering thought-provoking and unconventional experiences for the audience. From avant-garde plays to cutting-edge dance and music productions, Ilkhom Theatre provides a platform for artists to explore new forms of expression.

The theater features a mix of local and international talent, fostering a dynamic and diverse creative environment. Local actors, dancers, musicians, and playwrights collaborate with international artists, resulting in unique and cross-cultural productions. This fusion of talent brings a global perspective to the local stage, offering audiences a rich and immersive theatrical experience.

Ilkhom Theatre offers an intimate setting, creating a closer connection between the performers and the audience. The theater's cozy seating arrangement allows for an immersive experience, where every gesture, emotion, and expression can be witnessed up close. This intimate atmosphere enhances the audience's engagement with the performances, creating a more personal and memorable experience.

Ilkhom Theatre not only focuses on performances but also promotes artistic collaboration and education. The theater hosts workshops, masterclasses, and collaborative projects that engage local artists, aspiring actors, and theater enthusiasts. These initiatives contribute to the growth and development of the theater community in Uzbekistan and nurture emerging talents.

Opera Lounge Bar and Havana Club

After an evening of cultural exploration, Tashkent offers stylish lounges where visitors can unwind and enjoy a vibrant nightlife scene. The Opera Lounge Bar and Havana Club are two popular establishments that provide a relaxed and lively atmosphere, offering a selection of cocktails, live music, and entertainment. Here's a detailed exploration of these venues:

The Opera Lounge Bar is an elegant and sophisticated establishment, known for its stylish ambiance and upscale offerings. The bar offers a wide selection of classic and signature cocktails, expertly crafted by skilled mixologists. Visitors can savor their drinks while enjoying live music performances, creating a refined and enjoyable evening.

Havana Club, as the name suggests, captures the vibrant spirit of Cuba with its lively atmosphere and Latin-inspired entertainment. The club features a dance floor where visitors can sway to the rhythm of salsa, bachata, and other Latin beats. The bar serves a variety of cocktails, including the famous Cuban mojito, allowing guests to immerse themselves in a lively and energetic atmosphere.

Respecting Local Customs and Regulations

While enjoying the nightlife scene in Tashkent, it is important to respect local customs and regulations. Uzbekistan follows a more modest approach to nightlife compared to some other major cities. It is advisable to dress appropriately, adhere to local laws and regulations, and be mindful of cultural sensitivities. By respecting the local customs, visitors can fully appreciate and enjoy the nightlife scene in Tashkent while maintaining cultural awareness.

The Ilkhom Theatre and the Opera Lounge Bar and Havana Club offer distinct experiences in the realm of performing arts and nightlife. Whether you are seeking thought-provoking theater performances or a vibrant and stylish ambiance to unwind, Tashkent provides options that cater to diverse interests. Remember to check the schedules and plan your visit accordingly to make the most of the vibrant cultural and nightlife offerings in the city.

As you explore Tashkent, immerse yourself in its rich cultural tapestry, taste the local flavors, and embrace the warmth of the Uzbek people.

The city offers a delightful blend of ancient traditions and modernity, providing a captivating experience for every traveler.

CHAPTER THREE

Samarkand: The Jewel of Uzbekistan

Samarkand, often referred to as the "Jewel of Uzbekistan," is a city that epitomizes the grandeur of the Silk Road and the rich cultural heritage of Central Asia. Located in the northeastern part of Uzbekistan, Samarkand holds a significant place in history and is renowned for its breathtaking architecture, captivating history, and vibrant atmosphere. Here's an introduction to the enchanting city of Samarkand:

Historical Significance:

With a history spanning over 2,700 years, Samarkand has witnessed the rise and fall of empires, the passage of merchants, and the exchange of ideas along the ancient Silk Road. It has been a melting pot of cultures and civilizations, including Persians, Greeks, Arabs, Mongols, and Timurids, each leaving their indelible mark on the city's cultural landscape. Samarkand served as the capital of the powerful Timurid Empire, known for its architectural and artistic splendor.

Samarkand, with its rich Islamic architecture and vibrant cultural heritage, stands as a testament to the artistic achievements of Central Asia. The city's buildings showcase a harmonious blend of Central Asian, Persian, and Islamic architectural styles, creating a visual spectacle that captivates visitors. Here's a closer look at Samarkand's Islamic architecture and its cultural heritage:

Islamic Architecture

Samarkand is renowned for its Islamic architecture, which is characterized by exquisite tilework, geometric patterns, and intricate calligraphy. The buildings in the city, such as the madrasas, mosques, and mausoleums, display a remarkable attention to detail and artistic craftsmanship. The intricate tile mosaics, often featuring floral motifs and geometric designs, adorn the facades of these structures, creating a mesmerizing display of color and pattern. The azure domes and ornate minarets further enhance the architectural beauty, providing a visual feast for visitors.

The architectural styles in Samarkand reflect the influences of Central Asian, Persian, and Islamic traditions. The city's location along the Silk Road facilitated the exchange of ideas, cultures, and artistic techniques, resulting in a fusion of architectural elements. Central Asian influences can be seen in the use of colorful tilework and geometric patterns, while Persian influences are evident in the elegant domes and arches. Islamic architectural elements, such as calligraphy and geometric designs, are integrated throughout the city, emphasizing the religious and cultural significance of these structures.

Samarkand's cultural heritage extends beyond its architectural splendor. The city is a hub of traditional arts and crafts that have been practiced for centuries. Silk weaving, in particular, holds a special place in Samarkand's cultural heritage. The city is known for its exquisite silk textiles, crafted with intricate designs and vibrant colors. Visitors can witness the process of silk production and explore workshops where artisans create beautiful textiles using traditional techniques.

Embroidery is another traditional art form that thrives in Samarkand. Intricate patterns and motifs are meticulously stitched onto fabrics, creating stunning pieces of embroidered artwork. Ceramics also play a significant role in the city's cultural heritage, with master ceramicists producing intricate tiles and pottery adorned with colorful patterns.

Samarkand is also renowned for its miniature painting, a delicate art form that showcases intricate details and rich colors on a small scale. Miniature paintings often depict scenes from folklore, epic tales, or historical events, providing glimpses into the city's cultural and artistic traditions.

Visitors to Samarkand can immerse themselves in the city's cultural heritage by exploring workshops, markets, and bazaars where these traditional arts and crafts are showcased and sold. The city's cultural festivals and performances offer opportunities to experience traditional music, dance, and theater, providing a deeper understanding of Samarkand's vibrant cultural traditions.

Samarkand's Islamic architecture and cultural heritage create a captivating atmosphere that transports visitors back in time. The intricate tilework, geometric patterns, and artistic expressions reflect the city's rich cultural legacy and the artistic achievements of the region. Exploring Samarkand's architectural wonders and experiencing its traditional arts and crafts allows visitors to delve into the heart of Central Asian culture, appreciating the beauty, craftsmanship, and cultural traditions that define this enchanting city.

Architectural Marvels in Samarkand

Samarkand, the Jewel of Uzbekistan, is renowned for its extraordinary architectural treasures that have stood the test of time. These majestic structures reflect the city's rich cultural and historical heritage. Here's a closer look at some of Samarkand's most remarkable architectural marvels:

Registan Square

Registan Square is undoubtedly one of the most iconic landmarks in Samarkand. This vast public square is framed by three awe-inspiring madrasas, creating a stunning architectural ensemble. The three madrasas - Ulugbek, Sher-Dor, and Tilya-Kori - each exhibit unique design elements and intricate tilework. The facades of these Islamic schools are adorned with geometric patterns, calligraphy, and vibrant colors, showcasing the craftsmanship and artistry of the Timurid era. The grand arches, majestic domes, and minarets add to the grandeur of Registan Square, making it a breathtaking sight that captures the essence of Samarkand's architectural splendor.

Bibi-Khanym Mosque

The Bibi-Khanym Mosque, named after Timur's Chinese wife, was once one of the largest and most magnificent mosques in the Islamic world. Constructed in the 15th century, the mosque's design is a testament to the grandeur and architectural prowess of the Timurid dynasty. Though partially ruined, the remaining structure still showcases the mosque's former glory, with its massive entrance portal, intricately carved marble columns, and towering blue domes. The sheer scale and ornate decorations of the mosque leave visitors in awe of its past grandeur.

Shah-i-Zinda Necropolis

The Shah-i-Zinda Necropolis is a sacred complex that houses a series of mausoleums and tombs. It is considered one of the most sacred sites in Samarkand. The necropolis is built along a steep hillside and is adorned with vibrant blue-tiled facades. Each mausoleum has its unique architectural style and decoration, displaying a blend of Islamic, Persian, and Central Asian influences. The highlight of Shah-i-Zinda is the mausoleum of Kusam ibn Abbas, a cousin of Prophet Muhammad, which is a site of pilgrimage for Muslims. The intricate tilework, ornamental motifs, and the spiritual ambiance make Shah-i-Zinda a truly mesmerizing and spiritually significant place.

Gur-e-Amir Mausoleum

The Gur-e-Amir Mausoleum is the final resting place of Amir Timur, also known as Tamerlane, the great conqueror who established the Timurid Empire. This mausoleum is a masterpiece of Timurid architecture, featuring a grand dome, exquisite tilework, and intricate marble carvings. The interior of the mausoleum is equally impressive, with a stunning mosaic ceiling and beautifully decorated walls. The Gur-e-Amir Mausoleum stands as a testament to the architectural brilliance of the Timurid era and serves as a symbol of Timur's power and legacy.

These architectural marvels in Samarkand are not just remarkable structures; they are a living testament to the city's glorious past and the cultural achievements of the Timurid Empire. Exploring these architectural gems allows visitors to immerse themselves in the rich history, exquisite craftsmanship, and artistic vision that have shaped Samarkand into the mesmerizing city it is today. The awe-inspiring beauty, intricate designs, and historical significance of these structures make a visit to Samarkand an unforgettable experience.

Historical Sites and Museums in Samarkand

Samarkand, with its rich history dating back thousands of years, is home to a wealth of historical sites and museums that offer a glimpse into the city's illustrious past. These sites and museums provide invaluable insights into Samarkand's scientific achievements, ancient civilizations, and cultural heritage. Here are some notable historical sites and museums in Samarkand:

Ulugbek Observatory

The Ulugbek Observatory is a testament to Samarkand's scientific achievements during the Timurid era. Built in the 15th century by the renowned astronomer and mathematician Ulugbek, the observatory was a center of astronomical research and study. It housed one of the largest astronomical instruments of its time, the Samarkand Observatory, which was used to make precise astronomical observations and compile astronomical tables. Although only a portion of the original observatory remains, it serves as a reminder of Samarkand's contributions to the field of astronomy.

Afrosiab Museum

The Afrosiab Museum is dedicated to the ancient city of Afrasiab, which was once a bustling urban center and capital of the Sogdian civilization. The museum showcases artifacts and archaeological findings from Afrasiab, providing insights into the city's rich history, culture, and daily life. Visitors can explore exhibits displaying pottery, jewelry, coins, and murals that reflect the artistic and cultural achievements of this ancient civilization. The museum also features a detailed model of Afrasiab, offering a visual representation of the city as it existed centuries ago.

Samarkand Museum

The Samarkand Museum is a treasure trove of historical artifacts that delve into the city's history and cultural heritage. The museum exhibits a diverse collection of objects spanning various periods, including artifacts from the prehistoric era, the Silk Road era, and the Timurid dynasty. Visitors can explore displays of ceramics, textiles, weaponry, coins, and manuscripts, providing a comprehensive overview of Samarkand's historical significance. The museum also houses a gallery dedicated to the life and achievements of Amir Timur (Tamerlane), showcasing his legacy and impact on the city.

Registan Archaeological Site

The Registan Archaeological Site, located in the heart of Samarkand, is an important historical complex that has witnessed centuries of architectural and cultural development. The site encompasses several structures, including the ancient city center, the remnants of a medieval market square, and the remains of a 6th-century citadel. Excavations at the site have revealed ancient city walls, foundations of buildings, and artifacts that shed light on the city's early history and urban planning.

These historical sites and museums in Samarkand provide a fascinating journey through the city's past, from its scientific advancements to the remnants of ancient civilizations. Exploring these sites and museums allows visitors to gain a deeper understanding of Samarkand's historical and cultural significance, appreciating the legacy that has shaped the city into the cultural gem it is today. Whether it's exploring ancient ruins or marveling at centuries-old artifacts, Samarkand offers a captivating experience that takes visitors on a journey through time.

Savoring Local Cuisine

Samarkand, known for its rich history and architectural splendor, also offers a culinary scene that tantalizes the taste buds with a delightful array of flavors. Influenced by Persian, Central Asian, and Middle Eastern cuisines, the local food in Samarkand is a celebration of aromatic spices, succulent meats, and hearty flavors. Exploring the bustling bazaars and local eateries allows visitors to experience the authentic taste of Samarkand's cuisine. Here are some local specialties to savor:

Samarkand Plov

Samarkand Plov is a beloved national dish of Uzbekistan, and it holds a special place in the city's culinary scene. This flavorful rice pilaf is prepared by cooking rice with succulent pieces of meat, such as lamb or beef, along with aromatic spices like cumin, coriander, and turmeric. The dish is often garnished with fried onions, carrots, and raisins, adding a touch of sweetness to the savory flavors. Samarkand Plov is traditionally cooked in large cauldrons, creating a communal and festive dining experience.

Shashlik

Shashlik is a popular grilled meat dish that is a true delight for meat lovers. Skewered pieces of tender lamb or beef are marinated in a mixture of spices, including garlic, black pepper, and paprika, before being grilled over an open flame. The result is juicy and succulent meat with a smoky aroma. Shashlik is often served with fresh bread, grilled vegetables, and tangy sauces, creating a flavorful and satisfying meal.

Uzbek Pastries

Samarkand is known for its mouthwatering pastries that make for a delightful snack or dessert. One popular pastry is "Samsa," a baked triangular pastry filled with meat, potatoes, or vegetables. The flaky crust and flavorful fillings make it a favorite among locals and visitors alike. Another delightful pastry is "Chak-Chak," made from dough that is fried and coated with honey, creating a sweet and crunchy treat. These pastries can be found in local bakeries and street food stalls, offering a taste of the city's culinary heritage.

Bazaars and Local Eateries

Exploring the bustling bazaars and local eateries is a must-do for food enthusiasts in Samarkand. The Siyob Bazaar is a vibrant market where one can find an abundance of fresh produce, aromatic spices, and local ingredients. Here, visitors can experience the sights, sounds, and flavors of Samarkand, and even sample traditional snacks and street food. The bustling atmosphere and variety of food options make it a memorable culinary experience.

Samarkand's culinary scene not only satisfies the appetite but also provides a cultural experience. The flavors, spices, and traditional cooking methods reflect the city's cultural heritage and the influence of the Silk Road. Savoring the local cuisine allows visitors to immerse themselves in the vibrant culinary traditions of Samarkand, creating lasting memories of the city's delectable flavors and warm hospitality.

Visiting Samarkand is like stepping back in time to a city that has witnessed the rise and fall of civilizations, and yet continues to captivate with its architectural grandeur and cultural richness. The historical sites, vibrant bazaars, and warm hospitality of its people create an unforgettable experience that transports visitors to a bygone era. Samarkand truly stands as the Jewel of Uzbekistan, shining brightly with its architectural splendor and cultural heritage.

Bukhara: A Living Museum

Bukhara, often referred to as a "Living Museum," is a city that exudes history, culture, and architectural splendor. Located in the western part of Uzbekistan, Bukhara has a rich past as a vital center along the Silk Road, attracting merchants, scholars, and travelers from far and wide. Stepping into Bukhara is like entering a time capsule, where ancient traditions and architectural marvels blend seamlessly with modern life. Here's an overview of the captivating city of Bukhara:

Bukhara, with a history spanning over 2,000 years, holds immense historical significance as a vibrant center of trade, scholarship, and cultural exchange along the Silk Road. Its strategic location along major trade routes made it a melting pot of diverse cultures, ideas, and goods from East and West. Throughout its history, Bukhara thrived under the rule of various empires, leaving behind a legacy that can be seen in its architectural treasures and cultural heritage.

During the Persian Empire, Bukhara played a crucial role as a regional capital and a center of Persian culture. The city flourished as a center of learning and arts, attracting scholars, poets, and artists from far and wide. Its reputation as an intellectual hub persisted during the Arab conquest when Bukhara became a significant center of Islamic learning, housing renowned educational institutions and attracting scholars and theologians.

Bukhara's historical significance continued to flourish during the Mongol Empire when it served as an important administrative and cultural center. The Mongols recognized Bukhara's importance and preserved its traditions and institutions while incorporating their own administrative systems. The city became a hub of trade and craftsmanship, and its architectural landscape began to evolve, showcasing a blend of Persian, Central Asian, and Mongol influences.

The zenith of Bukhara's power and influence came during the Timurid dynasty, led by the great conqueror Amir Timur (Tamerlane). Timur transformed Bukhara into a magnificent capital, embellishing the city with grand architectural structures and fostering a flourishing artistic and cultural scene. The Timurid era marked a golden age for Bukhara, with the construction of magnificent mosques, madrasas, and mausoleums that have stood the test of time.

Architectural Splendor

Bukhara is renowned for its architectural splendor, which stands as a testament to its rich historical legacy. The city's skyline is adorned with towering minarets, majestic domes, and elaborate facades, creating a visually stunning panorama that evokes awe and admiration.

The Kalon Minaret, also known as the Tower of Death, is a towering masterpiece that dominates the city's skyline. Standing at around 47 meters tall, the minaret features intricate brickwork and ornamental designs, showcasing the architectural expertise of the craftsmen of the time. Its elegant proportions and intricate geometric patterns make it an iconic symbol of Bukhara's architectural grandeur.

The Po-i-Kalyan Complex, located in the heart of Bukhara, is another architectural gem that leaves visitors mesmerized. The complex includes the Kalyan Mosque, one of the largest mosques in Central Asia, and the

Mir-i-Arab Madrasa, an educational institution that has been active for centuries. The complex features stunning tilework, intricate carvings, and beautifully proportioned spaces, creating an enchanting ambiance that transports visitors to a bygone era.

The Ark Fortress, a historic citadel located within the city, offers a glimpse into Bukhara's military past and serves as a reminder of its importance as a political and administrative center. The fortress features imposing walls, gates, and towers, providing a fascinating insight into Bukhara's fortification strategies and architectural prowess.

These are just a few examples of the architectural splendor that graces Bukhara's landscape. The city is dotted with numerous mosques, madrasas, mausoleums, and palaces, each displaying intricate tilework, geometric patterns, and elaborate designs. The craftsmanship and attention to detail exhibited in these structures reflect the wealth, power, and influence that Bukhara held throughout its history.

Cultural Heritage

Bukhara is a city deeply rooted in its cultural heritage. It has been a center of Islamic learning, and many renowned scholars and theologians have emerged from its esteemed educational institutions. The city's traditional arts and crafts, such as ceramics, woodworking, embroidery, and carpet weaving, have been passed down through generations. Visitors can explore workshops and markets to witness the craftsmanship of local artisans and bring home exquisite handmade souvenirs.

Hospitality and Traditional Values

Bukhara is known for its warm hospitality and the preservation of traditional values. The locals embrace their cultural heritage, and traditional customs and rituals are still observed in daily life. The ancient concept of "mehmonxona," or guesthouse, is prevalent in Bukhara, where visitors are welcomed with open arms and provided with a comfortable and hospitable environment. This genuine hospitality adds to the charm of exploring Bukhara and interacting with its friendly residents.

UNESCO World Heritage Sites

Bukhara, with its rich cultural and historical heritage, is home to several UNESCO World Heritage Sites that embody the city's exceptional significance. These sites showcase the architectural treasures and cultural heritage that make Bukhara a true gem of Central Asia. Here are some notable UNESCO World Heritage Sites in Bukhara:

1. Historic Centre of Bukhara:

The Historic Centre of Bukhara encompasses the heart of the city and serves as a living testimony to its rich history. The site includes a vast array of well-preserved architectural monuments, such as mosques, madrasas, mausoleums, and trading domes. These structures, dating back to different periods, reflect the city's vibrant past as a center of trade, scholarship, and cultural exchange along the Silk Road. The Historic Centre of Bukhara provides an immersive experience, allowing visitors to wander through the winding streets and soak in the enchanting atmosphere of this UNESCO World Heritage Site.

2. Samanid Mausoleum

The Samanid Mausoleum, located in Bukhara, is a remarkable architectural masterpiece that dates back to the 10th century. It is one of the oldest surviving structures from the Samanid dynasty, which played a crucial role in the region's history. The mausoleum exhibits a unique architectural style, blending pre-Islamic motifs with Islamic elements. Its elegant simplicity, intricate brickwork, and geometric patterns are a testament to the artistic and architectural achievements of the time. The Samanid Mausoleum stands as a symbol of Bukhara's cultural and historical significance.

3. Kalyan Minaret and Mosque Complex

The Kalyan Minaret and Mosque Complex is an iconic landmark that dominates the skyline of Bukhara. The complex includes the Kalyan Mosque, one of the largest and most significant mosques in Central Asia. Its origins can be traced back to the 12th century, and it has since undergone renovations and additions. The minaret, known as the Tower of Death, stands adjacent to the mosque and showcases exceptional architectural beauty. Its intricate brickwork, decorative bands, and geometric patterns make it a true masterpiece. The Kalyan Minaret and Mosque Complex represent the religious and cultural importance of Bukhara throughout history.

Exploring these UNESCO World Heritage Sites in Bukhara takes visitors on a journey back in time, allowing them to witness the architectural brilliance, cultural richness, and historical significance of the city. The sites provide a deep understanding of Bukhara's role as a center of trade, learning, and spiritual enlightenment along the Silk Road. They offer an opportunity to appreciate the intricate tilework, elegant proportions, and artistic expressions that have shaped Bukhara into the captivating destination it is today.

Spiritual and Cultural Centers

Bukhara, often referred to as a city of spiritual and cultural significance, is home to numerous mosques, madrasas, and mausoleums that have played vital roles in Islamic learning, religious devotion, and cultural preservation. These spiritual and cultural centers not only showcase the architectural beauty of Bukhara but also provide a deeper understanding of the city's rich religious traditions and cultural heritage. Here are some notable examples:

1. Kalyan Mosque:

The Kalyan Mosque, also known as the Great Mosque of Bukhara, is one of the most significant and iconic mosques in Central Asia. Located within the Kalyan Mosque Complex, it has stood as a spiritual center for worshipers for over 1,000 years. The mosque's origins date back to the 12th century, although it has undergone renovations and expansions over the centuries. The grand courtyard, towering minarets, and stunning architectural details make it a remarkable sight to behold. Inside the mosque, visitors can experience the serene atmosphere and witness the beautiful calligraphy and decorative elements that adorn the prayer halls.

2. Mir-i-Arab Madrasa:

Adjacent to the Kalyan Mosque, the Mir-i-Arab Madrasa stands as a testament to the city's dedication to Islamic education. Established in the 16th century, it continues to serve as an active educational institution to this day. The madrasa's architecture is a stunning example of Bukhara's cultural heritage, with its intricately carved wooden doors, vibrant tilework, and mesmerizing domes. The interior courtyard is adorned with peaceful gardens and arched walkways, creating a tranquil space for contemplation and study.

3. Bolo-Hauz Complex:

The Bolo-Hauz Complex, located near the Ark Fortress, is a historical and spiritual center in Bukhara. At its heart is the Bolo-Hauz Mosque, a magnificent wooden mosque built in the 18th century. Its distinctive features include intricately carved columns and a beautiful wooden ceiling. The complex also encompasses a charming pool, surrounded by trees and reflecting the mosque's elegant architecture. The Bolo-Hauz Complex provides a serene and picturesque setting for spiritual reflection and prayer.

4. Abdulaziz-Khan Madrasa:

The Abdulaziz-Khan Madrasa, built in the 17th century, is another notable spiritual and cultural center in Bukhara. It is distinguished by its intricate tilework, blue domes, and elaborately decorated façade. The madrasa once served as a place of learning, providing education in various fields of Islamic studies. Today, it continues to impress visitors with its architectural beauty and serves as a venue for exhibitions and cultural events.

Exploring these spiritual and cultural centers allows visitors to delve into Bukhara's rich religious traditions, architectural beauty, and cultural heritage. The intricate tilework, grand domes, and exquisite details reflect the city's dedication to Islamic learning and its artistic achievements. The serene atmosphere within these centers offers a tranquil space for contemplation and a deeper understanding of Bukhara's spiritual significance. By immersing themselves in these cultural and religious landmarks, visitors can truly appreciate the heritage and legacy that continue to shape Bukhara's identity.

Exploring the Old Town (Shahristan)

The Old Town, also known as Shahristan, is the pulsating heart of Bukhara and a captivating destination for history enthusiasts and culture seekers. Stepping into the Old Town is like stepping back in time, as it immerses visitors in a bygone era of architectural marvels, bustling bazaars, and a vibrant atmosphere. Here is a glimpse into the enchanting experience of exploring the Old Town of Bukhara:

Labi Hauz Complex (Lyab-i Hauz):

At the heart of the Old Town lies the Labi Hauz Complex, a central square that revolves around a beautiful pond, or hauz, surrounded by historic buildings. The centerpiece of the complex is the Nadir Divan-Begi Madrasa, an architectural gem adorned with intricate tilework and elaborate motifs. The surrounding area is brimming with traditional teahouses, restaurants, and handicraft shops, creating a lively ambiance. Visitors can relax at one of the outdoor cafes, savoring the flavors of local cuisine while enjoying the serene atmosphere by the water's edge.

Ancient Streets and Architectural Gems:

Wandering through the labyrinthine streets of the Old Town, visitors encounter a wealth of ancient buildings, each with its own story to tell. The narrow lanes are lined with centuries-old houses, mosques, madrasas, and mausoleums, showcasing Bukhara's rich architectural heritage. The ornate facades, intricate tilework, and elaborate wooden carvings bear witness to the city's cultural and artistic accomplishments. Walking along these ancient streets, visitors can explore historic sites such as the Magoki-Attori Mosque, the Poi Kalyan Complex, and the Chor Minor, each offering unique insights into Bukhara's history and cultural identity.

Bustling Bazaars and Handicrafts:

The Old Town of Bukhara is renowned for its bustling bazaars, where vibrant colors, enticing aromas, and a plethora of goods create a sensory feast for visitors. The domed trading halls, known as tokis, are filled with stalls selling traditional handicrafts, spices, textiles, carpets, and souvenirs. The atmosphere is alive with the sounds of bargaining and the bustling activities of local merchants. Exploring the bazaars allows visitors to immerse themselves in the vibrant market culture and witness the skilled craftsmanship of local artisans.

Residential Neighborhoods:

As visitors stroll through the Old Town, they have the opportunity to catch glimpses of everyday life in Bukhara. Residential neighborhoods with their traditional houses, courtyards, and shaded alleyways offer an authentic glimpse into the local community's daily routines and traditions. Observing the intricacies of local life, from women embroidering colorful textiles to children playing in the streets, adds depth to the exploration of the Old Town, creating a sense of connection with the city's living heritage.

Exploring the Old Town of Bukhara is like stepping into a living museum, where history, culture, and architectural splendor come together. It allows visitors to immerse themselves in the vibrant past of this ancient city, meandering through its narrow streets, discovering hidden corners, and encountering architectural treasures at every turn. The bustling bazaars, the timeless ambiance, and the glimpses of everyday life create an unforgettable experience that truly captures the essence of Bukhara's rich history and cultural heritage.

Traditional Music and Dance

Bukhara is known for its vibrant traditional music and dance performances, which offer a glimpse into the cultural heritage of the region. Local musicians and dancers showcase their talents in various venues, such as teahouses and cultural centers. The melodies of traditional string instruments, like the dutar and tanbur, fill the air, while graceful dances, including the traditional Bukhara dance, captivate audiences with their elegance and charm. Experiencing a traditional music and dance performance in Bukhara provides a memorable and immersive cultural experience.

Bukhara is a city that transports visitors to a bygone era, where history, culture, and architectural beauty intertwine. Exploring the city's UNESCO World Heritage Sites, spiritual and cultural centers, and the enchanting Old Town allows visitors to immerse themselves in Bukhara's rich heritage. The warm hospitality, traditional values, and captivating traditional music and dance make Bukhara a truly unforgettable destination.

Khiva

Khiva, a UNESCO World Heritage Site, is a true gem of Uzbekistan, offering visitors a journey back in time to the era of Silk Road caravans and ancient desert cities. Nestled in the remote desert region of Khorezm, Khiva is a well-preserved oasis of history and culture. Stepping into Khiva is like stepping into a fairy tale, with its labyrinthine streets, majestic minarets, and ornate architectural wonders. Here's an introduction to the enchanting city of Khiva:

Khiva is often referred to as a living museum, and for good reason. The city has preserved its historic core, known as Ichan-Kala, in remarkable condition. Its mud-brick walls and architectural treasures transport visitors to a bygone era, where the echoes of the past can still be felt in every corner. Khiva's authenticity and well-preserved heritage make it a unique and captivating destination for travelers seeking a glimpse into Uzbekistan's rich history.

Khiva's Historic Architecture

Khiva is a treasure trove of historic architecture, where each structure tells a story of the city's rich cultural and architectural heritage. From towering minarets to grand palaces, Khiva's architecture reflects a fusion of Islamic, Persian, and Central Asian influences. The attention to detail, exquisite craftsmanship, and harmonious blend of decorative elements make Khiva a captivating destination for architectural enthusiasts. Here are some notable examples of Khiva's historic architecture:

1. Kalta-Minor Minaret:

The Kalta-Minor Minaret is a remarkable architectural marvel that stands out for its unique blue mosaic tiles and truncated design. Constructed in the 19th century by Muhammad Amin Khan, the minaret was intended to be much taller, but its construction was halted, leaving it at its current height of approximately 29 meters. The minaret's intricate tilework and vibrant colors create a striking contrast against the desert landscape, making it an iconic symbol of Khiva's architectural ambition.

2. Juma Mosque:

The Juma Mosque, dating back to the 10th century, is a sight to behold with its mesmerizing forest of intricately carved wooden columns. The mosque's interior is adorned with over two hundred intricately carved pillars, each displaying unique patterns and designs. The play of light and shadow, along with the rhythmic repetition of the columns, creates an enchanting atmosphere within the mosque. The exterior of the mosque, with its plain brickwork, offers a stark contrast to the opulence found inside.

3. Tash-Hauli Palace:

The Tash-Hauli Palace, also known as the Stone House, is an architectural masterpiece that showcases the grandeur of Central Asian palace design. Built in the 19th century, the palace complex features majestic courtyards, intricately carved wooden pillars, and vibrant tilework. The harem, with its ornate rooms and lavish decorations, offers a glimpse into the opulent lifestyle of Khiva's rulers. The palace complex also includes reception halls, administrative buildings, and a beautiful garden, creating a serene and regal ambiance.

4. Muhammad Amin Khan Madrasa:

The Muhammad Amin Khan Madrasa is a grand Islamic school that bears the name of its patron, Muhammad Amin Khan. Built in the early 19th century, the madrasa stands as a testament to the architectural splendor of Khiva. Its facade is adorned with intricate tilework, geometric patterns, and calligraphy. The inner courtyard features beautiful arched walkways and a tranquil atmosphere, providing a glimpse into the scholarly and religious life of the past.

Exploring Khiva's historic architecture is like stepping into a living museum, where each structure tells a unique story of the city's rich cultural heritage. The intricate tilework, ornate carvings, and harmonious architectural designs create a feast for the eyes, transporting visitors to a bygone era of artistic excellence and grandeur. Khiva's architectural treasures not only showcase the city's past glory but also inspire a sense of awe and wonder among those who have the opportunity to experience them firsthand.

Ichan-Kala: The Inner City

Ichan-Kala, the inner city of Khiva, is a remarkable architectural ensemble that transports visitors to the heyday of the Silk Road. Enclosed within massive fortress walls, Ichan-Kala is a living testament to Khiva's rich history and cultural heritage. The narrow streets and bustling squares of Ichan-Kala lead visitors on a journey through time, unveiling the architectural splendor and captivating stories of the past.

The intricate maze-like layout of Ichan-Kala beckons visitors to explore its hidden corners and discover its architectural treasures. Every street, every alleyway, and every courtyard holds surprises, with each turn revealing another architectural marvel. The atmosphere of Ichan-Kala is palpable, evoking a sense of stepping back in time to an era when Khiva was a thriving center of trade, culture, and intellectual pursuits.

Walking through the streets of Ichan-Kala, visitors are greeted by a mesmerizing array of monuments, including mosques, madrasas (Islamic schools), mausoleums, and palaces. Each structure showcases exquisite craftsmanship, intricate tilework, and ornate carvings that bear witness to Khiva's artistic and architectural prowess.

The Juma Mosque, with its forest of intricately carved wooden columns, stands as a testament to the city's religious heritage and architectural ingenuity. The minarets that rise above the city's skyline, such as the Islam-Khoja Minaret and the Kalta-Minor Minaret, offer breathtaking views and reflect the city's aspirations for spiritual and architectural greatness.

The Muhammad Amin Khan Madrasa, with its ornate tilework and captivating calligraphy, provides a glimpse into the world of Islamic education and scholarly pursuits in Khiva's past. The Tash-Hauli Palace, with its grand courtyards, delicate wooden pillars, and vibrant tilework, transports visitors to the opulent lifestyle of Khiva's rulers.

As visitors wander through Ichan-Kala, they encounter bustling bazaars, where local artisans display their craftwork, and traditional Uzbek handicrafts, such as ceramics, textiles, and carpets, are on full display. The aroma of freshly baked bread wafts through the air, tempting visitors to taste the local delicacies and immerse themselves in the vibrant market culture.

Every step in Ichan-Kala reveals layers of history and culture, creating an immersive experience that brings the past to life. The combination of architectural splendor, atmospheric streets, and vibrant marketplaces makes Ichan-Kala a truly unique and unforgettable destination.

Ichan-Kala's significance as a UNESCO World Heritage Site lies not only in its architectural treasures but also in its ability to transport visitors to a bygone era. It serves as a living reminder of Khiva's glorious past and offers a glimpse into the rich cultural tapestry that continues to shape the city's identity. Exploring Ichan-Kala is a journey of discovery, where history, art, and culture converge to create an experience that captivates the senses and leaves a lasting impression.

Museums and Cultural Institutions

In addition to its architectural wonders, Khiva is home to several museums and cultural institutions that offer a deeper understanding of the city's history, art, and cultural heritage. These institutions provide visitors with the opportunity to explore Khiva's rich past and gain insights into its significance as a center of intellectual and artistic achievements. Here are some notable museums and cultural institutions in Khiva:

State Museum of Khorezm History

Located within the walls of Ichan-Kala, the State Museum of Khorezm History offers a comprehensive overview of the region's ancient history. The museum showcases a remarkable collection of artifacts, archaeological finds, and exhibits that provide a glimpse into the Khorezm civilization, which thrived in this area during ancient times. Visitors can explore displays of pottery, ancient coins, jewelry, and other artifacts that shed light on the daily life, culture, and achievements of the Khorezmian people.

Islam Khodja Minaret and Museum

The Islam Khodja Minaret, one of Khiva's iconic landmarks, also houses a museum that offers insights into the city's Islamic art, calligraphy, and historical artifacts. Visitors can climb to the top of the minaret, where they are rewarded with panoramic views of Khiva's skyline and the surrounding area. The museum exhibits a diverse collection of Islamic art, including manuscripts, ceramics, and textiles, providing a deeper understanding of the artistic and cultural heritage of the region.

Within these museums and cultural institutions, visitors can delve into the stories and legacies of Khiva, gaining a greater appreciation for the city's rich history and cultural significance. These venues not only preserve and showcase valuable artifacts but also contribute to the preservation and promotion of Khiva's cultural heritage, ensuring that future generations can continue to appreciate and learn from the city's past.

When visiting Khiva, travelers have the opportunity to experience the renowned Uzbek hospitality that is deeply rooted in the culture and traditions of the region. The locals take pride in their warm and welcoming nature, and visitors are often greeted with genuine smiles and open arms.

One of the best ways to experience traditional Uzbek hospitality is by staying in a traditional guesthouse known as a "khona." These guesthouses are often family-run establishments that offer a glimpse into the local way of life. The hosts go above and beyond to ensure the comfort and satisfaction of their guests, treating them as honored members of the family.

Staying in a khona allows visitors to immerse themselves in the authentic Uzbek lifestyle. Guests are treated to traditional Uzbek meals, which showcase the rich flavors and unique culinary traditions of the region. From aromatic pilafs and hearty soups to flavorful kebabs and freshly baked bread, each meal is a delightful culinary experience.

Beyond the delicious food, guests have the opportunity to engage in conversations with their hosts, who are eager to share stories, traditions, and local insights. These interactions provide a deeper understanding of the Uzbek way of life and offer a genuine connection to the local community.

The warmth and generosity of the Uzbek people extend beyond the khonas. Whether wandering through the streets of Khiva or exploring its attractions, visitors are often greeted with smiles and friendly gestures. Locals may strike up conversations, offer recommendations, or even invite visitors into their homes for tea or snacks, showcasing their genuine hospitality.

Uzbek hospitality is not just about providing comfort and nourishment to guests; it is about creating a sense of belonging and building lasting connections. Visitors to Khiva have the opportunity to experience this firsthand, creating memories and friendships that will endure long after their departure.

It is important for travelers to reciprocate this warm hospitality by showing respect for local customs and traditions. Learning a few basic phrases in the Uzbek language, such as greetings and expressions of gratitude, can go a long way in fostering positive interactions and showing appreciation for the local culture.

Experiencing traditional Uzbek hospitality in Khiva is a truly enriching and heartwarming experience. It allows visitors to go beyond the surface attractions and connect with the soul of the city, forging genuine connections with the local community and creating cherished memories that will last a lifetime.

Festivals and Events

Khiva is a city that cherishes and celebrates its rich cultural heritage through a variety of festivals and events. These vibrant occasions offer visitors a chance to experience traditional music, dance, crafts, and culinary delights, providing an immersive and unforgettable cultural experience. Here are some notable festivals and events that take place in Khiva:

Silk and Spices Festival

One of the most eagerly anticipated events in Khiva is the Silk and Spices Festival, held annually in May. This festival celebrates the historical significance of the Silk Road and the vital role Khiva played as a center of trade and cultural exchange. During the festival, the streets of Khiva are transformed into a colorful and lively stage, adorned with traditional decorations and bustling with activity.

Visitors can witness captivating performances of traditional music, dance, and theater, showcasing the cultural diversity of the region.

Artisans from across Uzbekistan gather to showcase their exquisite craftsmanship, offering a wide range of handmade goods, including textiles, ceramics, jewelry, and traditional Uzbek costumes. The aroma of spices fills the air as food stalls serve up a tantalizing array of traditional Uzbek delicacies, allowing visitors to indulge in the flavors of the Silk Road.

The Silk and Spices Festival is not only a celebration of the past but also a vibrant showcase of the living traditions and creative talents of the local community. It offers a unique opportunity to immerse oneself in the cultural fabric of Khiva and create lasting memories.

Other Cultural Events and Festivals

Throughout the year, Khiva hosts a variety of cultural events and festivals that showcase the region's diverse heritage. These events often feature music concerts, dance performances, traditional craft exhibitions, and culinary showcases.

Music enthusiasts can enjoy performances of traditional Uzbek music, including classical maqom music, folk songs, and instrumental ensembles. These melodic performances provide a captivating glimpse into the rich musical heritage of the region, with mesmerizing rhythms and soul-stirring melodies.

Dance performances offer a feast for the eyes, as skilled dancers bring traditional Uzbek dances to life. The graceful movements, vibrant costumes, and intricate choreography reflect the cultural diversity and artistic excellence of Uzbekistan's dance traditions.

Art exhibitions and craft showcases provide visitors with an opportunity to witness the exceptional skills of local artisans. Traditional crafts such as pottery, carpet weaving, embroidery, and miniature painting are displayed, allowing visitors to appreciate the intricate techniques and the artistic beauty of these handmade creations.

Food festivals and culinary events highlight the flavors and culinary traditions of Khiva and the wider region. Visitors can sample a variety of traditional dishes, from savory plov and hearty soups to delicate pastries and refreshing beverages. These culinary experiences offer a delightful exploration of the local cuisine and its vibrant flavors.

Attending these festivals and events in Khiva allows visitors to witness the living traditions, artistic expressions, and cultural diversity that make the city truly special. The lively atmosphere, vibrant performances, and immersive experiences create cherished memories and provide a deeper appreciation for the rich cultural heritage of Khiva and Uzbekistan as a whole.

Khiva offers a captivating journey into a fairy tale-like world of ancient architecture, rich history, and cultural heritage. From its well-preserved old city to its museums, cultural institutions, and warm hospitality, Khiva invites visitors to step back in time and immerse themselves in the enchanting ambiance of this UNESCO World Heritage Site.

CHAPTER FOUR
Exploring Other Regions
Nukus and the Savitsky Museum

Nukus, the capital city of the autonomous Republic of Karakalpakstan in Uzbekistan, is a hidden gem for art enthusiasts and cultural explorers. While it may not be as well-known as other cities in Uzbekistan, Nukus offers a unique experience, particularly through its renowned Savitsky Museum.

The Savitsky Museum, officially known as the State Art Museum of the Republic of Karakalpakstan, is a true treasure trove of art and culture. It was founded by Igor Savitsky, a Russian artist and collector, who dedicated his life to preserving and showcasing the forbidden Soviet-era avant-garde art that was suppressed and hidden during Stalin's reign.

The museum houses an impressive collection of over 90,000 artworks, including paintings, sculptures, ceramics, textiles, and archaeological artifacts. The collection is a testament to Savitsky's relentless efforts to save these artworks from destruction and to showcase the diverse cultural heritage of the region.

The museum's exhibition halls display an extensive range of artwork, including works by Russian avant-garde artists such as Alexander Volkov, Ural Tansykbaev, and Victor Ufimtsev. The collection also features Karakalpakstan folk art, regional archaeological finds, and a significant collection of Uzbek traditional costumes.

One of the highlights of the Savitsky Museum is its impressive collection of Russian avant-garde art, which includes works from the 1920s and 1930s. These artworks provide a unique insight into the creativity and experimentation of artists during this tumultuous period in Soviet history. Visitors can admire the bold colors, abstract compositions, and innovative techniques used by these artists.

Beyond its art collection, the museum also features a library and research center dedicated to the study and preservation of the cultural heritage of Karakalpakstan and Central Asia as a whole. Scholars, researchers, and art enthusiasts from around the world are drawn to the museum to explore its extensive resources and delve deeper into the history and artistic traditions of the region.

Nukus itself offers a glimpse into the daily life and culture of Karakalpakstan. The city's streets are lined with Soviet-era architecture, and its bazaars bustle with local traders selling fruits, vegetables, and traditional crafts. Visitors can also explore the nearby Mizdahkan Necropolis, an ancient burial site that provides a fascinating insight into the region's past.

A visit to Nukus and the Savitsky Museum is a unique and enriching experience that offers a different perspective on art, history, and cultural heritage. It is an opportunity to appreciate the resilience of artistic expression and to discover the hidden artistic gems that were preserved against all odds.

Fergana Valley and Crafts

The Fergana Valley is a picturesque region located in eastern Uzbekistan, known for its stunning landscapes, fertile farmland, and rich cultural heritage. The valley is renowned for its traditional crafts, which have been passed down through generations and continue to thrive in local communities. Here is all you need to know about the Fergana Valley and its vibrant craft traditions:

The Fergana Valley is nestled between the Tian Shan and Pamir-Alay mountain ranges, creating a scenic backdrop of rolling hills, lush green fields, and meandering rivers. It is a fertile region, famous for its agricultural production, particularly fruits, vegetables, and cotton.

The Fergana Valley is celebrated for its traditional crafts, which reflect the skills and artistry of the local artisans. Here are some of the prominent crafts in the region:

1. Silk Weaving: The valley is renowned for its silk production and intricate silk weaving techniques. Margilan, a city in the Fergana Valley, is known for its silk workshops and the production of exquisite silk fabrics, including ikat patterns. Visitors can witness the intricate process of silk production and explore silk bazaars where a wide range of silk products, such as scarves, clothing, and accessories, are available for purchase.

2. Pottery: The Fergana Valley is also famous for its pottery traditions. Artisans create beautiful ceramic vessels, plates, and decorative items using traditional techniques. Visitors can witness the pottery-making process, visit workshops, and even try their hand at shaping clay under the guidance of skilled potters.

3. Woodcraft: The valley is home to skilled woodcraft artisans who produce intricate wood carvings, furniture, and musical instruments. The artistry of these craftsmen is evident in the delicate designs and attention to detail seen in their creations. Visitors can explore woodcraft workshops and observe the artisans at work, or purchase unique wooden pieces as souvenirs.

4. Handmade Textiles: The Fergana Valley is a hub for traditional textile production, including embroidery, felting, and weaving. Local women excel in intricate embroidery techniques, creating beautiful patterns on fabrics and garments. Felting is another traditional craft in the valley, with artisans producing felt carpets and decorative items. Visitors can observe the process of textile making, interact with artisans, and purchase handmade textiles of exceptional quality.

The Fergana Valley is dotted with craft centers and workshops where visitors can witness the crafts firsthand and even participate in workshops to learn the traditional techniques. These centers provide insights into the history, techniques, and cultural significance of the crafts and offer opportunities to engage with local artisans.

Kokand, a city in the Fergana Valley, is particularly known for its craft workshops and traditional arts. The city boasts several craft centers where visitors can witness the production of silk, pottery, woodcrafts, and textiles. These centers often provide demonstrations and offer workshops where visitors can try their hand at these traditional crafts.

Exploring the Fergana Valley

Travelers can explore the Fergana Valley by visiting its cities and towns, each known for its distinct craft traditions. In addition to Kokand and Margilan, Andijan is another city worth visiting for its crafts and historical sites. The valley is also dotted with bazaars and local markets, where artisans showcase and sell their crafts, providing visitors with ample opportunities to appreciate and purchase traditional Fergana Valley crafts.

The Fergana Valley and its crafts offer a fascinating glimpse into Uzbekistan's cultural heritage and artistic traditions. Exploring the region allows travelers to witness the skill and creativity of local artisans, learn about traditional craft techniques, and bring home unique handmade souvenirs that capture the essence of this beautiful and culturally rich part of Uzbekistan.

Termez: Ancient City on the Silk Road

Termez, located in southern Uzbekistan, is an ancient city with a rich history dating back over 2,500 years. Situated along the historic Silk Road, Termez was a vital trading hub and a center of cultural exchange between East and West. Here is all you need to know about Termez and its historical significance:

Termez has been inhabited by various civilizations, including the Greeks, Persians, Kushans, Arabs, and Mongols, each leaving their mark on the city's cultural heritage. It was a significant center of Buddhist and Islamic culture, and its strategic location made it a coveted city throughout history.

Archaeological Sites

Termez is renowned for its numerous archaeological sites that showcase its rich past. Some of the notable sites include:

1. Buddhist Archaeological Sites: The region around Termez is home to several ancient Buddhist monasteries and stupas. The Fayaz Tepe Buddhist Temple, located just outside the city, features remnants of Buddhist structures and sculptures dating back to the 1st century AD. This site provides insights into the spread and influence of Buddhism in the region.

2. Kyrk-Kyz Fortress: This ancient fortress, located in the outskirts of Termez, dates back to the 9th century. The fortress consists of a labyrinth of rooms, corridors, and watchtowers, reflecting the defensive architecture of the time. Visitors can explore the fortress and enjoy panoramic views of the surrounding area.

3. Termez Archaeological Museum: The Termez Archaeological Museum houses a remarkable collection of artifacts excavated from the region. The museum showcases relics from different historical periods, including Kushan and Islamic artifacts, pottery, sculptures, and coins. It offers visitors a comprehensive understanding of the region's history and cultural heritage.

Islamic Heritage

Termez is also known for its Islamic heritage, with several important religious sites that highlight the city's significance as a center of Islamic learning. Some notable sites include:

1. Hakim at-Termezi Mausoleum: This mausoleum is dedicated to the famous Sufi mystic and poet, Hakim at-Termezi. It is a revered pilgrimage site for Muslims and showcases beautiful Islamic architectural elements, including intricate tilework and geometric designs.

2. Sultan Saodat Ensemble: This complex consists of several mausoleums of the Sayyids, descendants of Prophet Muhammad. The mausoleums feature stunning turquoise domes and intricate tilework, making it a visually striking site.

Aside from its archaeological and religious sites, Termez offers unique cultural experiences that provide a glimpse into local traditions and lifestyle. Visitors can explore local bazaars, interact with friendly locals, and enjoy traditional Uzbek cuisine.

Termez is also known for its melon production, and tasting the locally grown sweet melons is a must-do when visiting the city. Additionally, traditional music and dance performances, showcasing local folk traditions, can be enjoyed at cultural events and festivals.

Termez is blessed with beautiful natural surroundings, including the Amu Darya River and the Karakum Desert. Visitors can take a leisurely stroll along the riverbanks, enjoy sunset views, or even take a boat ride to witness the scenic beauty of the region.

Termez offers a captivating blend of history, culture, and natural beauty. Exploring its archaeological sites, experiencing its Islamic heritage, and immersing oneself in the local traditions make for an unforgettable journey back in time. With its strategic location on the Silk Road and its diverse cultural heritage, Termez offers a unique perspective on Uzbekistan's ancient past and its enduring cultural traditions.

Tian Shan Mountains

The Tian Shan Mountains, located in Central Asia and spanning across several countries, including Uzbekistan, offer a breathtaking backdrop for outdoor enthusiasts and nature lovers. Here is all you need to know about outdoor adventures in the Tian Shan Mountains:

The Tian Shan Mountains are a majestic mountain range known for their stunning peaks, deep valleys, glacial lakes, and alpine meadows. The range extends through Uzbekistan's eastern regions, offering a variety of outdoor activities and breathtaking landscapes to explore.

Hiking and Trekking

The Tian Shan Mountains provide an excellent opportunity for hiking and trekking enthusiasts. There are numerous trails of varying difficulty levels, ranging from gentle walks through alpine meadows to challenging multi-day treks that lead to high mountain passes. Some popular hiking destinations include:

1. Chimgan Mountains: Located near Tashkent, the Chimgan Mountains offer a range of hiking options suitable for both beginners and experienced hikers. Trails in this area often lead to stunning viewpoints, mountain lakes, and picturesque valleys.

2. Ugam-Chatkal National Park: Situated in the western Tian Shan Mountains, Ugam-Chatkal National Park is a haven for outdoor activities. The park features diverse landscapes, including dense forests, mountainous terrain, and stunning waterfalls. Hikers can explore the park's trails and discover hidden natural gems along the way.

Skiing and Winter Sports

The Tian Shan Mountains provide excellent opportunities for winter sports enthusiasts. The region receives abundant snowfall during winter, making it a popular destination for skiing, snowboarding, and other winter activities. Some notable ski resorts in the area include:

1. Beldersay Ski Resort: Located in the Chimgan Mountains near Tashkent, Beldersay is a popular ski resort with well-groomed slopes suitable for both beginners and advanced skiers. The resort offers ski rental facilities and instructors for those new to skiing.

2. Charvak Ski Resort: Situated near the Charvak Reservoir, Charvak Ski Resort offers a range of winter sports activities, including skiing, snowboarding, and tubing. The resort provides equipment rental services and has slopes suitable for different skill levels.

Mountaineering and Climbing

For those seeking more adventurous pursuits, the Tian Shan Mountains offer opportunities for mountaineering and climbing. Experienced climbers can challenge themselves with ascents to the region's peaks, such as:

1. Khan Tengri: Standing at an impressive height of 7,010 meters, Khan Tengri is one of the highest peaks in the Tian Shan range. Scaling this peak requires technical climbing skills and experience in high-altitude mountaineering.

2. Peak Lenin: Located on the border between Kyrgyzstan and Tajikistan, Peak Lenin is a popular destination for mountaineers. With an elevation of 7,134 meters, it attracts climbers from around the world.

Wildlife and Nature Exploration

The Tian Shan Mountains are home to a diverse range of flora and fauna. Wildlife enthusiasts can explore the region's national parks and nature reserves, where they may encounter rare and endangered species. Some of the notable wildlife species include snow leopards, ibex, Marco Polo sheep, and golden eagles.

Nature lovers can also indulge in activities such as birdwatching, nature photography, and simply enjoying the tranquility of the mountainous landscapes.

Safety Considerations

When engaging in outdoor activities in the Tian Shan Mountains, it is important to prioritize safety. Here are some considerations:

1. Proper equipment: Ensure you have appropriate hiking or climbing gear, including sturdy footwear, warm clothing, navigation tools, and safety equipment.

2. Weather conditions: Be aware of changing weather conditions and pack accordingly. Check weather forecasts before heading out and be prepared for sudden changes in mountain weather.

3. Physical fitness: Assess your fitness level and choose activities that are suitable for your abilities. Start with easier trails and gradually progress to more challenging hikes or climbs.

4. Local guidance: If you're unfamiliar with the area or new to certain activities, consider hiring a local guide or joining organized tours for a safer and more enjoyable experience.

The Tian Shan Mountains offer a playground for outdoor adventurers, with a range of activities to suit all levels of experience and interests. Whether you're seeking a leisurely hike through scenic landscapes or an adrenaline-pumping climb to towering peaks, the Tian Shan Mountains provide unforgettable experiences amidst the beauty of nature.

Aral Sea

The Aral Sea, once one of the largest inland bodies of water in the world, has faced significant environmental challenges over the past few decades. Here is all you need to know about the Aral Sea and the environmental issues it has encountered:

Geography and History

The Aral Sea is located between Uzbekistan and Kazakhstan in Central Asia. It was once a thriving ecosystem, providing a vital water source for the surrounding communities and supporting a rich biodiversity. However, the sea has experienced a dramatic decline in water levels and has been greatly affected by human intervention and environmental degradation.

Environmental Challenges

1. Water Diversion: The primary cause of the Aral Sea's decline is the diversion of its two main tributary rivers, the Amu Darya and Syr Darya, for irrigation purposes. These rivers have been heavily tapped for agricultural irrigation, resulting in a significant reduction in the inflow of freshwater into the Aral Sea. As a result, the sea has shrunk in size, leading to a loss of its unique ecosystem.

2. Salinity and Pollution: With the shrinking of the Aral Sea, the concentration of salts and pollutants in the remaining water has significantly increased. The exposed seabed has become highly saline and contaminated with chemicals and pesticides, posing a threat to the health of aquatic life and local communities.

3. Loss of Biodiversity: The environmental degradation of the Aral Sea has resulted in the loss of diverse species of fish, plants, and wildlife that once thrived in the region. The decline of the sea has disrupted the natural balance of the ecosystem and caused irreversible damage to its biodiversity.

4. Socioeconomic Impacts: The shrinking of the Aral Sea has had severe socioeconomic consequences for the communities that relied on it for their livelihoods. The fishing industry has collapsed, leaving thousands of people unemployed, and agricultural productivity has been affected by the loss of water resources.

Efforts for Restoration and Conservation

Recognizing the severity of the environmental crisis facing the Aral Sea, efforts have been made to address and mitigate its effects. Here are some initiatives:

1. The Aral Sea Basin Program: This program, initiated by the governments of Uzbekistan and Kazakhstan, aims to restore and sustainably manage the Aral Sea and its surrounding ecosystems. It focuses on water management, improving agricultural practices, and promoting sustainable development in the region.

2. Reforestation Projects: Afforestation and reforestation initiatives have been undertaken in the Aral Sea region to stabilize the soil, prevent desertification, and improve the overall ecological conditions. Planting drought-resistant trees and shrubs helps to restore the ecosystem and mitigate the effects of wind erosion.

3. International Support: The international community, including organizations such as the World Bank and the United Nations, has provided support and funding for projects aimed at the restoration of the Aral Sea. These initiatives focus on improving water management practices, promoting sustainable agriculture, and implementing conservation measures.

CHAPTER FIVE
Practical Tips and Advice
Safety and security

Personal Safety:

- Stay aware of your surroundings and exercise caution, especially in crowded areas or tourist attractions.

- Keep your belongings secure and be mindful of pickpockets. Use a money belt or secure bag to carry your valuables.

- Avoid walking alone at night, especially in dimly lit or unfamiliar areas.

- Follow local laws and regulations, and respect the customs and traditions of the local population.

- Familiarize yourself with the emergency contact numbers and the location of the nearest embassy or consulate.

Health and Medical:

- Ensure that you have travel insurance that covers medical expenses, including emergency medical evacuation.

- Carry necessary medications and a first aid kit for minor injuries or illnesses.

- Drink bottled water or purified water to avoid water-borne diseases. Avoid consuming tap water or ice from unknown sources.

- Consider getting vaccinations or consulting a healthcare professional before traveling to Uzbekistan, based on your personal health condition and the recommended vaccines.

Transportation Safety:

- Use licensed and reputable transportation services, such as registered taxis or official transportation companies.

- Follow safety guidelines while using public transportation, including buses, trains, and metros.

- Be cautious when crossing roads, as traffic conditions can be challenging in some areas. Use pedestrian crossings and follow traffic signals.

- If renting a vehicle, familiarize yourself with local traffic rules and regulations.

Natural Disasters:

- Uzbekistan is prone to earthquakes and occasional floods. Stay informed about weather conditions and follow local authorities' instructions in case of any natural disasters or severe weather events.

- If hiking or engaging in outdoor activities, be aware of potential risks, such as extreme weather conditions or wildlife encounters. Take necessary precautions and be prepared with appropriate gear.

Emergency Situations:

- In case of an emergency, dial the local emergency number (112) or seek assistance from the nearest police station or medical facility.

- Register with your embassy or consulate upon arrival to receive updates and assistance during your stay.

It's important to note that while Uzbekistan is generally considered safe for tourists, it's always wise to exercise common sense, be aware of your surroundings, and take necessary precautions to ensure a safe and enjoyable trip.

Local Customs and Etiquette

When visiting Uzbekistan, it's important to be aware of the local customs and etiquette to show respect to the culture and traditions. Here are some key points to keep in mind:

1. Greetings and Respect:

- Uzbekistanis value politeness and respect. Greet people with a warm smile and a handshake. When meeting someone for the first time, it's customary to address them with their full name and use honorifics if applicable.

- Show respect to elders and people in positions of authority. It's common to greet them first and use formal language and titles when speaking to them.

- Public displays of affection, especially between couples, are generally not common in Uzbek culture. It's advisable to exercise restraint in this regard.

2. Clothing:

- Uzbekistan is a predominantly Muslim country, and it's respectful to dress modestly, especially when visiting religious sites. Both men and women should cover their shoulders and legs.

- Women may choose to wear loose-fitting clothes that cover their arms, legs, and chest. Wearing a scarf or shawl to cover the head is not mandatory unless visiting mosques.

- Men typically wear trousers or long pants and avoid sleeveless shirts.

3. Religious Sites and Customs:

- When visiting mosques, it's important to dress modestly and remove your shoes before entering. Women may be required to cover their hair with a scarf or head covering.

- Show respect by refraining from loud conversations, photography without permission, or any behavior that may disturb worshippers.

- During the holy month of Ramadan, when Muslims fast from sunrise to sunset, it's polite to refrain from eating, drinking, or smoking in public spaces during daylight hours.

4. Dining and Food Etiquette:

- Uzbek cuisine is diverse and delicious, and it's customary to try local dishes. When dining with locals, it's polite to taste a bit of everything offered to show appreciation for the hospitality.

- Wash your hands before and after meals. Traditionally, meals in Uzbekistan are eaten with hands, but utensils may also be provided.

- It's customary to wait for the host or eldest person at the table to begin eating before you start.

- Finish all the food on your plate to show appreciation for the meal.

- When visiting someone's home, it's customary to bring a small gift, such as sweets or fruits, as a gesture of gratitude.

5. Photography:

- Always ask for permission before taking photographs of individuals, especially in more conservative areas or when photographing religious sites.

- Some sites may charge an additional fee for photography or prohibit photography altogether. Respect the rules and guidelines provided by the authorities.

6. Language and Communication:

- Learn a few basic phrases in Uzbek or Russian to greet locals and show your interest in their culture. Locals appreciate the effort to communicate in their language.

- When communicating, maintain a polite and respectful tone. Avoid raising your voice or using offensive language.

7. Tipping:

- Tipping is not mandatory in Uzbekistan, but it's appreciated for good service. It's customary to leave a small tip in restaurants, cafes, and for services provided by guides or drivers. The amount is generally around 10% of the total bill.

By observing these customs and practicing respectful behavior, you will create a positive impression and have a more immersive and rewarding experience during your visit to Uzbekistan.

Weather and Best Time to Visit

The weather in Uzbekistan varies throughout the year, and the best time to visit depends on your preferences and the activities you plan to engage in. Here is some detailed information about the weather and the recommended times to visit Uzbekistan:

1. Spring (March to May):

Spring is a beautiful time to visit Uzbekistan, as the weather is mild and pleasant. The temperatures gradually rise, with March being cooler and May becoming warmer. The landscapes are lush and vibrant, with blooming flowers and blossoming trees. It's a great time for outdoor activities and exploring historical sites without extreme heat. However, it's advisable to pack some warm clothing as evenings can still be cool.

2. Summer (June to August):

Summer in Uzbekistan is characterized by hot and dry weather. The temperatures can soar, particularly in July and August, with daytime temperatures reaching well above 35°C (95°F) in some areas. It's a good time to visit if you can handle the heat and plan your activities accordingly. If you visit during summer, it's recommended to carry sunscreen, a hat, sunglasses, and drink plenty of water to stay hydrated.

The evenings are relatively cooler and more comfortable for outdoor exploration.

3. Autumn (September to November):

Autumn is another favorable season to visit Uzbekistan. The temperatures start to drop in September, providing relief from the summer heat. October and November offer pleasant weather with mild temperatures, making it an ideal time for sightseeing, outdoor activities, and exploring the beautiful landscapes. The autumn foliage adds a touch of beauty to the scenery, particularly in the mountainous regions. It's advisable to bring a light jacket or sweater for cooler evenings.

4. Winter (December to February):

Winter in Uzbekistan can be cold, especially in the northern and mountainous regions. Temperatures can drop below freezing, and snowfall is common, particularly in December and January. However, if you enjoy winter activities, such as skiing or experiencing the beauty of snow-covered landscapes, visiting during this time can be rewarding. Cities like Tashkent and Samarkand are milder compared to the mountainous areas. It's essential to pack warm clothing, including coats, hats, gloves, and layers to stay comfortable.

The best time to visit Uzbekistan ultimately depends on your preferences and the activities you plan to undertake. Spring and autumn are generally considered the most pleasant seasons, offering comfortable temperatures for exploring historical sites, enjoying outdoor activities, and experiencing the local culture. Summer can be hot but manageable if you plan your activities accordingly and take precautions against the heat. Winter is ideal for those seeking winter sports or a unique experience in a snow-covered landscape.

It's advisable to check the weather forecasts before your trip and pack accordingly to ensure your comfort and enjoyment throughout your stay in Uzbekistan.

Money-Saving Tips

When traveling to Uzbekistan, here are some money-saving tips that can help you make the most of your budget:

1. Plan your trip during the shoulder season: Consider visiting Uzbekistan during the spring (March to May) or autumn (September to November) when the weather is pleasant, and tourist demand is lower. Prices for accommodations and flights tend to be more affordable during these periods.

2. Stay in budget accommodations: Look for budget-friendly accommodations such as guesthouses, hostels, or smaller hotels that offer reasonable rates. These options often provide comfortable and clean accommodations at a fraction of the cost of luxury hotels.

3. Eat at local restaurants and street food stalls: Explore local eateries and street food stalls where you can savor authentic Uzbek cuisine at a lower cost. These places often offer delicious meals at affordable prices, allowing you to experience the local flavors without breaking the bank.

4. Use public transportation: Utilize public transportation options like buses, metros, or shared taxis (marshrutkas) to get around the cities. They are generally cheaper than private taxis and offer a chance to experience local transportation. Just ensure that you are aware of the routes and schedules.

5. Bargain at bazaars and markets: When shopping at traditional bazaars and markets, don't hesitate to bargain for a better price. It's a common practice in Uzbekistan, and you can often get discounts on souvenirs, textiles, handicrafts, and other items.

6. Explore free or low-cost attractions: Uzbekistan is rich in historical and cultural attractions, some of which are free or have minimal entrance fees. Take advantage of these sites to explore the country's heritage without spending too much.

7. Carry a reusable water bottle: Instead of buying bottled water, carry a reusable water bottle and refill it at filtered water stations or purchase purified water from local shops. This helps reduce plastic waste and saves you money on buying multiple bottles of water.

8. Research and book in advance: Research and book your accommodations, flights, and activities in advance to take advantage of early bird discounts or promotional offers. Booking in advance can often help secure better deals and avoid last-minute price hikes.

9. Learn basic phrases in Uzbek or Russian: Learning a few basic phrases in Uzbek or Russian can go a long way in interacting with locals and negotiating prices, as it shows your interest in the local culture and can potentially lead to better deals.

10. Be mindful of your expenses: Keep track of your spending and stick to a budget. Avoid unnecessary splurges and prioritize your activities and experiences. By being mindful of your expenses, you can make your money last longer and make the most of your trip.

By implementing these money-saving tips, you can have a rewarding and budget-friendly experience while exploring the wonders of Uzbekistan.

Sample Itineraries

3-day cultural and spiritual itinerary for solo travelers in Uzbekistan

Day 1: Tashkent - Spiritual Exploration

- Start your day by visiting the Khast Imam Square, home to the iconic Khast Imam Mosque and the Muyi Muborak Library, which houses the world's oldest Quran.

- Explore the Chorsu Bazaar, a bustling traditional market where you can immerse yourself in the local culture and find unique souvenirs.

- Visit the State Museum of History of Uzbekistan to delve into the country's rich cultural heritage.

- In the evening, attend a performance at the Ilkhom Theatre to experience contemporary Uzbek theater and artistic expressions.

Day 2: Samarkand - Architectural Marvels

- Take a high-speed train from Tashkent to Samarkand (around 2 hours).

- Start your exploration at the Registan Square, marveling at the grandeur of the three madrasas and the intricate tilework.

- Visit the Shah-i-Zinda Necropolis, a sacred site with stunning mausoleums and a spiritual ambiance.

- Explore the Bibi-Khanym Mosque and the Gur-e-Amir Mausoleum, both architectural masterpieces.

- End the day at the Ulugbek Observatory, an ancient site of astronomical observation.

Day 3: Bukhara - Ancient Oasis

- Travel from Samarkand to Bukhara (around 3-4 hours by train or car).

- Begin your day at the Ark Fortress, a historic citadel with panoramic views of the city.

- Visit the Po-i-Kalyan Complex, which includes the Kalyan Mosque and the Kalyan Minaret, known as the "Tower of Death."

- Explore the Labi Hauz Complex, a vibrant square surrounded by historical buildings and a central pond.

- End the day at the Chor Minor, a unique architectural gem with four minarets.

This itinerary allows you to experience the spiritual and cultural essence of Uzbekistan within a limited timeframe. It combines visits to significant spiritual sites, architectural marvels, and cultural landmarks, giving you a glimpse into the country's rich heritage. Remember to check the opening hours of attractions and plan your transportation accordingly.

7 days itinerary

Certainly! Here's a sample 7-day itinerary for your tour in Uzbekistan, along with estimated costs. Please note that the costs provided are approximate and can vary depending on your travel style, accommodation choices, dining preferences, and additional activities.

Day 1: Tashkent

- Arrive in Tashkent and transfer to your hotel.

- Explore the city's highlights, including Independence Square, Amir Timur Square, and the State Museum of History of Uzbekistan.

- Estimated cost:

  - Accommodation (mid-range hotel): $60-$80 per night

  - Meals: $15-$25 per day

  - Transportation: $5-$10 per day (local transportation)

Day 2: Samarkand

- Take a high-speed train from Tashkent to Samarkand.

- Visit the Registan Square, Gur-e-Amir Mausoleum, Bibi-Khanym Mosque, and Shah-i-Zinda Necropolis.

- Estimated cost:

  - Train ticket (economy class): $15-$25

  - Accommodation (mid-range hotel): $60-$80 per night

  - Meals: $15-$25 per day

  - Transportation: $5-$10 per day (local transportation)

Day 3: Samarkand

- Explore more of Samarkand, including the Ulugbek Observatory and the Afrosiab Museum.

- Visit the Samarkand Paper Workshop and the Siyob Bazaar for local crafts and souvenirs.

- Estimated cost:

  - Accommodation (mid-range hotel): $60-$80 per night

  - Meals: $15-$25 per day

  - Entrance fees: $10-$15 per attraction

  - Transportation: $5-$10 per day (local transportation)

Day 4: Bukhara

- Travel from Samarkand to Bukhara by train or private car.

- Visit the historic sites in Bukhara, such as the Ark Fortress, Po-i-Kalyan Complex, and Lyab-i Hauz.

- Explore the local markets and enjoy traditional Uzbek cuisine.

- Estimated cost:

  - Train ticket or private car transfer: $20-$30

  - Accommodation (mid-range hotel): $60-$80 per night

  - Meals: $15-$25 per day

  - Entrance fees: $10-$15 per attraction

  - Transportation: $5-$10 per day (local transportation)

Day 5: Bukhara

- Continue exploring Bukhara, including the Chor Minor, Sitorai Mokhi-Khosa Palace, and the Chor-Bakr Necropolis.

- Experience traditional music and dance performances in the evening.

- Estimated cost:

  - Accommodation (mid-range hotel): $60-$80 per night

  - Meals: $15-$25 per day

  - Entrance fees: $10-$15 per attraction

  - Transportation: $5-$10 per day (local transportation)

  - Performance ticket: $10-$20

Day 6: Khiva

- Travel from Bukhara to Khiva by train or private car.

- Explore the Ichan-Kala (inner city) of Khiva, including the Kalta-Minor Minaret, Juma Mosque, and Tash-Hauli Palace.

- Enjoy the traditional atmosphere and architectural beauty of the city.

- Estimated cost:

  - Train ticket or private car transfer: $20-$30

  - Accommodation (mid-range hotel): $60-$80 per night

  - Meals: $15-$25 per day

  - Entrance fees: $10-$15 per attraction

  - Transportation: $5-$10 per day (local transportation)

Day 7: Khiva and Return to Tashkent

- Explore more of Khiva, visiting the Mohammed Amin Khan Madrasa and the Islam Khodja Minaret.

- Return to Tashkent by flight or train.

- Estimated cost:

- Flight or train ticket: $50-$100

- Accommodation (mid-range hotel): $60-$80 per night

- Meals: $15-$25 per day

- Entrance fees: $10-$15 per attraction

- Transportation: $5-$10 per day (local transportation)

Estimated Total Cost for 7 days: $950-$1,400 (excluding international flights)

Please note that the estimated costs are based on mid-range accommodation and moderate spending on meals and activities. Actual costs can vary depending on your travel preferences and choices. It's advisable to budget for additional expenses, such as souvenirs, additional activities, and unforeseen costs.

Also, ensure to check the latest visa requirements and fees for your nationality before traveling to Uzbekistan.

Conclusion

As you reach the end of this travel guide, you have embarked on a remarkable journey through the enchanting land of Uzbekistan. From the bustling streets of Tashkent to the architectural wonders of Samarkand, Bukhara's living museum, and the fairy tale city of Khiva, you have experienced the rich tapestry of history, culture, and spirituality that this Central Asian gem has to offer.

Uzbekistan, with its captivating blend of ancient traditions and modern developments, has opened its doors to the world, inviting travelers to immerse themselves in its vibrant culture, architectural marvels, and warm hospitality. You have explored the remnants of the Silk Road, witnessed the artistic achievements of bygone eras, and savored the flavors of traditional Uzbek cuisine. The memories you have created and the stories you will tell will remain with you for a lifetime.

Beyond its historical and cultural riches, Uzbekistan has embraced the future with open arms. The country's commitment to sustainable tourism, preservation of cultural heritage, and the well-being of its people create a harmonious blend of old and new. As you have journeyed through this land, you have also witnessed the efforts made to protect the environment, support local communities, and ensure a memorable and responsible travel experience.

Uzbekistan, with its awe-inspiring landscapes, intricate architecture, and diverse cultural tapestry, has captured the hearts of travelers seeking a profound connection with the past. It has revealed itself as a living testament to the beauty and resilience of human civilization.

As you bid farewell to Uzbekistan, you carry with you the echoes of ancient civilizations, the vibrant colors of bazaars, and the warmth of Uzbek hospitality. May this guide serve as a cherished companion, inspiring you to return to this remarkable destination or embark on new adventures across the globe.

Remember, the world is vast and full of wonders, waiting to be explored. As you continue your travels, may you embrace the spirit of curiosity, respect for diverse cultures, and the joy of discovery.

Bon voyage, fellow traveler, and may your future journeys be filled with unforgettable experiences!

Safe travels and farewell from the captivating land of Uzbekistan.

Made in the USA
Las Vegas, NV
02 December 2023

81998502R00069